Divergent and
Philosophy

Popular Culture and Philosophy® Series Editor: George A. Reisch

For full details of all Popular Culture and Philosophy® books, visit www.opencourtbooks.com.

Popular Culture and Philosophy®

Divergent and Philosophy

The Factions of Life

Edited by
COURTLAND LEWIS

OPEN COURT
Chicago

Volume 94 in the series, Popular Culture and Philosophy ®, edited by George A. Reisch

To find out more about Open Court books, call toll-free 1-800-815-2280, or visit our website at www.opencourtbooks.com.

Open Court Publishing Company is a division of Carus Publishing Company, dba Cricket Media.

Copyright © 2016 by Carus Publishing Company, dba Cricket Media

First printing 2016

Printed and bound in the United States of America.

ISBN: 978-0-8126-9902-9

Library of Congress Control Number: 2015953178

Contents

Choose!

COURTLAND LEWIS

Choose! Your time for thinking is over. It's now time to pick where you'll spend the rest of your life, unless you fail, of course. If you fail, you'll be an outcast, with no "blood" or family. Choose! You're sixteen, you've been tested, you know what you're destined to become. Now, all you must do is . . . *Choose!*

Did you know what you wanted to be and do for the rest of your life, at age sixteen? I know there are a few of you out there who did, but for most of us, it takes a little longer. Some people decide when they get older, others never seem to figure it out. Some are forced into a certain way of life, while others stumble into their calling. Many choose the life they think will be the easiest, while a few, choose paths that are purposely difficult, with no guarantee of success.

Enter *Divergent and Philosophy*, which contains enough wisdom to make the highest ranking Erudite look like an initiate. Coupled with Veronica Roth's *Divergent* series, you'll have enough philosophical serums to ensure you survive and maybe even thrive in the real-world Choosing Ceremony called "life."

Divergent and Philosophy is the textbook for Divergents—Wisdom before Ignorance! We scoured the planet to bring together the most talented faction members, factionless, and even a few from the Bureau to analyze and discuss the Philosophy of *Divergent*. We discovered that the *Divergent* series presents a narrative that engages readers on every level, from moral and civic virtues to the proper order of society, from normalcy and being different to love, evil, and forgiveness. The most impressive thing about Roth's *Divergent* series is that it not only contains philosophical themes, but it actually does philosophy. In other words, it proposes hypotheses, tests them for consistency, and offers conclusions about what is true and wise. Once you understand these philosophical themes, you'll be better-equipped to resist the serums of our own world—you know, like ignorance, deception, and discrimination. If you can resist these, then maybe you can live a life and help the world achieve Roth's noble goal of peace.

Warning, Divergents Are Everywhere

Divergent and Philosophy examines the personal struggles that all people face from time to time: What sort of person should I be? What if I find out my life is a lie? What do I owe my parents? Am I normal?

The book also has its own "Choosing Ceremony," exploring ways to make life choices and to select the type of social order you believe most worthy of support. Some chapters examine each faction, looking at its virtues, vices, and other features that will help you pick the "right" one. These chapters give you a glimpse into what it's like to be faced with the most important decision of your life, the one that will forever determine who you are and where you belong.

For those who've read the books or seen the movies, future Chicago is on the verge of revolution, but is this the result of the faction system itself, or is it the people who are responsible for the social discord? We offer some insights into answering this question, looking at some influential philosophical arguments for how best to order society. Even if we answer this question, there are all sorts of questions remaining about whether America—or any country—is really much different from Roth's Chicago. The authors present strong evidence that'll have you thinking: Have I been slipped a serum all of my life? We also offer some lessons on how to recognize injustice and evil, and we suggest some different ways you might stand against them.

The Allegory of Chicago

If you haven't read all of the books or seen all of the movies, you're in for a surprise. It's a good surprise, so don't be scared.

Think of it as a journey through your own personal "fear land-scape," helping you find and overcome those things that prevent you from being free. As you begin your adventure with *Divergent and Philosophy*, you begin a journey of self-discovery and wisdom similar to Tris's. The process begins with self-reflecting on what's important in your life, and by trusting your own ability to make good decisions. This is where Tris Prior's journey began, and so too must yours.

Tris resembles Socrates (469–399 B.C.E.), the original Divergent. In the "Allegory of the Cave" (*Republic*, lines 514a–520a), Socrates likens the quest for knowledge and wisdom to a journey of self-discovery, from the dark shadows of a cave to the pure light of the sun. Imagine living in a cave, similar to the Dauntless cave, where the only things you can see are the dim reflections of shadows. If this were all you knew, you'd think these shadows were accurate representations of reality—they'd be your basis for truth. Now, imagine you get released and find your way outside, where the sun of "Truth" shines on everything. This would be a difficult journey, for it'd take time for your eyes to adjust and your mind to make sense of all of these new sights. After familiarizing yourself with the beauty of Truth, you should be motivated to return to the cave to share your discovery, in hopes the others will learn and become wiser. Sadly, upon returning, the others will probably laugh at you, or even try to kill you.

Tris's path is almost identical to Socrates's tale of discovery. She begins "chained" to social and familial expectations, deep within the "cave" of future Chicago's faction system. Her journey quickly moves her away from the relative safety of home, towards the danger of being Dauntless. Dauntless doesn't satisfy her thirst for truth, and before long she's driven further outside the "cave," where she discovers the real truth— Chicago's faction system is a lie! While other Chicagoans choose to ignore the truth, or blindly fight a war that distracts them from dealing with the truth, Tris tackles it head-on. As a result—spoilers!!!—she's tortured, imprisoned, and eventually killed for the truth.

Yes, Tris sometimes doubted herself, but even Socrates doubted himself: at age seventy, during the month between his conviction and execution, he tried his hand at being a poet, just in case that was his true purpose in life. Tris, after devising a plan to safely prevent the Bureau of Genetic Welfare from erasing the memories of all Chicagoans, reflects on her motivations and on whether or not it's acceptable to let Caleb sacrifice himself. We all know how it ends, and even though we might not like the outcome, Tris's decision is the wisest. Self-doubt, usually in the form of self-reflection, is the hallmark of a good critical thinker because it leads to wisdom, and wisdom is what we all should strive towards. It's the only way to escape the cave of ignorance, and Tris's willingness to risk it all to find truth is why we love her so much!

Time to Choose

Roth's *Divergent* series is about choice, so in the end, it's about life. Every choice you make, from what books you buy, what college you attend, and what person you marry, to telling your friend a lie, cheating on your taxes, or refusing to help someone you know who's in pain; every one of them determine who you are and what sort of life you'll live. The good news is, you don't always have to make the right decision. As long as you learn and grow from your mistakes, you'll become wiser. This is what Roth shows us with characters like Tris, Four, Caleb, and Peter.

So, if you don't know what faction you belong to that's okay. It takes many years for people to figure out exactly who they are and who they want to be. Philosophy is the love of wisdom, not the love of knowledge. Knowledge is something we can master and demonstrate with ease—think $2 + 2 = 4$. It gives us a sense of security and certainty. Wisdom, on the other hand, is something vastly different—think Tris trying to figure out who's good, who's evil, and what's the truth. Wisdom must be lived and experienced, and often, the more you learn the less you understand. The beauty of wisdom is that it inspires us to live better lives and to do what is right. It's not the knowledge of her character traits that makes Tris Divergent; it's her ability to self-reflect and look for choices based on the truth that makes her wise, and therefore, Divergent.

Just like Roth's Chicago, life might present you with a limited set of choices, whether they're Abnegation, Erudite, Amity, Dauntless, Candor, or something entirely different. In fact, life can sometimes make you feel like there are no choices, like the people of Chicago who thought being factionless was worse than death. If Roth, Tris, and *Divergent and Philosophy* don't teach anything else, you should learn that when life gives you no options, you have to create your own. To do this you must be wise and willing to work hard, especially when others start telling you you're going to fail.

Choose wisely, my fellow Divergent.

I

Are You
Divergent?

1
Drugging the Kids

JESSICA SEYMOUR

Divergent is a story about control. Control over young people, control over adults, and control over the social order. It's the fear of losing control which drives the power-holders in the series to resort to more and more oppressive means to keep the population in check.

One of the most invasive techniques of control is the use of serums: the medical method to keep the population compliant and obedient. While the majority of characters in the series are helpless against the serums, the Divergent can resist. As the Divergent become more active within the story, their ability to resist the serums that control the population becomes symbolic of their resistance to the corrupt power structure, which relies on their world's idea of what is "right" and "normal." As well as resisting the serums, young characters in the series are also shown using the serums and adapting them for their own purposes—such as when Tobias repeatedly goes back over his fear landscape, and when Peter erases his own memory during *Allegiant*.

The Divergent, who're immune to the serums' effects, are outside of the factions' control because the faction leaders can't force their preferred standard of behavior onto them. The serum-resistance of the Divergent creates an opportunity for the young reader to live vicariously through the characters, and empower themselves through a series of books which acknowledge their anxieties. As Vanessa Harbour has suggested, authors can produce a vicarious experience for young readers by taking them on a journey where the youth in the

3

fiction live through and overcome their oppression, and readers often develop a strong empathetic relationship with fictional characters whom they identify with. This is particularly true, in the case of the *Divergent* series, for young people who've been forced to submit to medication to quell those impulses and behaviors which are considered "divergent" from the cultural norm. By showing characters becoming powerful even in the face of repeated attempts to suppress their individuality, *Divergent* creates a vicarious experience of power and empowerment for the reader to engage with.

Real-World Methods of Medical Control

According to *US News and World Report*, in 2013, about 6.4 million children between four and seventeen were diagnosed and treated for ADHD in the US, despite there being no scientifically grounded test to identify the disorder. As Bob Jacobs claims, these diagnoses are just the personal judgments of doctors using various personality tests and the testimony of the child's parents and teachers. Michael Corrigan points out that the symptoms of ADHD include inattention, impulsivity and hyperactivity, which are shown by every child at one point or another. He also observes that the tests used to diagnose ADHD are often subjective, with physicians labeling and medicating the child after a few brief meetings: "a child can be diagnosed" with "a form[sic] of ADHD at the discretion of the ADHD expert . . . even if they do not display any of the symptoms."

One of the troubling aspects of this approach to ADHD is that when a young person is diagnosed with ADHD they're immediately given corrective treatment, which generally involves prescription medication designed to inhibit the "symptoms" of ADHD. The medications—or serums, however, can be harmful. For example, ADHD medication can often *cause* medical problems, including weight gain in adolescents (*US National Library of Medicine*), anxiety, and addiction (*US News and World Report*).

So how do we justify the mass-drugging of young people for "behavioral disorders" whose symptoms are so broad that virtually any child could be diagnosed with the disease? Why do adults feel that their medical interventions are necessary, when there's little evidence to suggest that a child's inattention is anything but ordinary child behavior? Why do we want to classify and medicate young people for failing to live up to what we believe a child "should" be?

ADHD medication makes it extremely difficult to exhibit the personality traits which adults find troubling—such as impulsivity or hyperactivity—and so by medicating young people who don't adhere to the adult ideal of "normal" behavior, we're creating a culture where abnormality or divergence from the norm is a disease. Studies into the prevalence of ADHD diagnoses without proper medical grounding, like the one from *US News and World Report*, show that parents could be pressuring doctors to diagnose their children in order to gain access to medication which will make their child easier to manage. Corrigan suggests parents, teachers, and doctors would rather simply label a child and medicate their difficult behaviors away, rather than address *why* the child behaves the way they do.

Other critics and scholars say that the trend of ADHD diagnoses in recent years is just a way to control young people by forcing them to behave a certain way. When a child does not fit into our subjective standards of normal, drugging them into compliance is easier than talking to them, trying to understand them or—heaven forbid—changing our own ideas about what it means to be "normal." Dr. Bob Jacobs, from the Youth Affairs Network of Queensland, writes that by defining ADHD as divergence from what we as a society have defined as "normal," we're giving ourselves licence to suppress whichever citizens—usually young people—who fail to comply:

> When the group in power begins to define deviance as 'disease', and drug people as a consequence, a very scary situation emerges. . . . We are not declaring you abnormal because you violate our subjective standards of normalcy and disrupt our neat little world; we are declaring you abnormal because the doctor says you are 'sick'.

When young people *diverge* from what is expected, when they become difficult to control, they're told that they are sick and given medicine to make them "better." This, then, is reflected in the stories they read. Storytelling is a way for people to examine their anxieties—to distance themselves from the real world at the same time that they are critiquing it. Given that medication as a form of control is so common in modern society—

6.4 million children is nothing to sneeze at—the fact that mass-drugging has found its way into literature for young people isn't surprising.

Enforcing the "Normal"

The adults in *Divergent* put a lot of stock in conformity, just like adults in the real world. They like to know that their factions will behave according to what is expected of them. Every faction has a set of specific character traits which each member is expected to embody, and if they can't do this successfully, then they risk becoming factionless: "To live factionless is not just to live in poverty and discomfort; it is to live divorced from society, separated from the most important thing in life: community." The fear of being cast out is what keeps the population obedient.

If people conform to an expected pattern of behavior—if they're easy to predict—then they are likewise easy to control. Jeanine Matthews tries to eliminate the Divergent because she fears losing the power she holds as leader of the Erudite. Other leaders like Joanna Reyes and Marcus Eaton also demand that the people of their factions conform to what is expected of them, and when the people in the factions fail to conform, then they're either drugged (Amity) or shamed (Abnegation) into behaving the way that their faction leaders expect. The Amity faction even bakes their peace serum into the bread, to limit the faction's capacity for violence or discontent. The serums, like the medication taken by children with ADHD, limit their range of emotions to what is acceptable or "normal" by the faction standards.

The faction serums control the population by forcing people to conform to faction ideals. This allows faction leaders to ensure complete control because the people in the factions cannot behave differently from the expected norm. While the Amity use their faction serum for control, the Dauntless and Candor factions use their serums to terrorize their young initiates; forcing terrifying hallucinations onto them with the simulation serum, and violating their privacy through the truth serum. Here, the serums are deliberately targeted towards young people who may not yet be completely obedient to the faction ideals. The serums force them to show bravery or honesty, and in this way they're taught what will be expected of them if they remain with the faction.

While the *Divergent* series shows clearly how people can be controlled and manipulated through medication, there's a group who can resist—the Divergent. They can fight the effects of the serums, and in this way they demonstrate to the young reader the importance of fighting back against oppression. There's a relationship in the series between wanting to fight back, and *actually* fighting back. Without the desire to fight, the Divergent are just as vulnerable to the serums as the others. The choice to fight is far more important than the *ability* to fight. This is particularly clear when the Amity drug Tris during *Insurgent*, and she fails to fight off the serum.

While Tris shows an extraordinary ability to resist the effects of serum, particularly truth serum and fear serum, the peace serum works perfectly on her. Tris is overdosed with the peace serum after fighting with Peter in the Amity compound, and experiences the euphoria and passivity typical of the Amity faction. She has no desire to fight the serum once it has taken effect: "I feel good. I feel a little like . . . like I'm floating. Or swaying." Later, when the serum has worn off, she's furious with the Amity for dosing her against her will, but can't explain why the serum affected her the way that it did. Tobias, ever observant, points out that perhaps the serum worked on her because she wanted it to: "Sometimes . . . people just want to be happy, even if it's not real." The takeaway from this is that there's a relationship between the methods power-holders use to control the population and the desire to conform or remove yourself from responsibility for your actions.

Joanna Reyes makes it clear that, if she had her way, she'd force the peace serum onto every member of the population to ensure their obedience to the Amity ideals: "If I could give the serum to everyone in this city, I would. You would certainly not be in the situation you are in now if I had." As noted by both Ed Jones and Hillary Conner, in their respective works, mass-drugging has been used in science fiction narratives before to illustrate the dangers of government medical intervention to create "perfect" humans, and these mass-druggings are always shown to have terrible consequences in the stories. Despite the obvious anger and mistrust felt by Tobias in the face of Tris's forced drugging, Joanna still believes that medication is in the best interests of the population.

As Jacobs describes, this is the same line of reasoning used by doctors and parents who drug children "for their own good," because their disobedience is a symptom of their "disease." The child isn't considered "responsible" for their behavior, and the parents or guardians aren't held accountable for the environment which the child is raised. They're just labelled and medicated to prevent further divergence. Instead of investigating *why* Tris attacks Peter, or why she feels that a physical attack is the best response to Peter's actions, she's overdosed on peace serum to prevent further outbursts. But this drugging would have been ineffective if Tris had not subconsciously wanted to stop feeling the pain and anger which prompted the attack.

Taking It Too Far . . .

The Bureau of Genetic Welfare maintains its control over experiments through surveillance and controlled intervention. When the Chicago experiment appears to be failing after the rebellion breaks out, the Bureau plans to use the memory serum from Abnegation to reset the experiment: "'Resetting' is our word for widespread memory erasure. . . . It is what we do when the experiments that incorporate behavioral modification are in danger of falling apart." So, in order to maintain the control they desire, the Bureau must destroy everything that makes their subjects unique. Essentially, they want to delete all of the inconvenient personality traits—aggression, discontent, rebelliousness—from the citizens of Chicago and start their personalities from scratch. The memory serum causes initial disorientation, followed by permanent memory loss. Similarly, as Jane Collingwood has shown, children on ADHD medication often report side-effects which include sluggishness, anxiety, and loss of appetite. Like the memory serum in *Divergent*, real-world attempts to suppress inconvenient personality traits have consequences which impact the subject's quality of life. Medication also limits a person's ability to express themselves or behave differently from their "normal" counterparts. *Divergent* extends this anxiety to a mass-destruction of personal identity.

The Bureau is portrayed as unashamedly inhumane in their treatment of the Chicago experiment and other experiments like it: "But why do they believe they have the right to rip people's memories, their identities, out of their heads, just because it's convenient to them?" While the justification for their actions may seem sensible, or even kind, the fact remains that their monstrous treatment of the human beings under their care is considered by Tris and the other Divergent to be a form of genocide. Likewise, the use of peace serum in the Amity faction is a violation of Tris's right to feel angry and hurt when Peter steals the hard drive containing footage of her parents' murders. The fact that Joanna Reyes would happily drug every single person in Chicago proves the potentially dangerous use of the serum as a means of controlling the population—eliminating their ability to feel certain emotions simply because the Amity faction doesn't approve of them. The ability of the power-holders in *Divergent* to limit what individuals think and feel is a negative consequence of a social order which relies on a narrow idea of "normal."

The Power of Choice

Tris's ability to resist serum leads her towards more active choices and deliberate expressions of agency as the series progresses. When the Erudite use their simulation serum to control the Dauntless faction, it's Tris's Divergence which makes her immune to their control and gives her the opportunity to stop them from wiping out the Abnegation faction. Tris's divergence from the norm—her ability to choose to act against what's expected of her—is what gives her the power to fight back against Jeanine Matthews's hostile takeover.

It allows her to resist the death serum at the end of *Allegiant*, because she trusts that the power she has as a Divergent character—the power to fight off serums when she wants to—will be enough to keep her alive: "I'm good at fighting off serums. There's a chance I'll survive." The power Tris wields allows her to deal a major blow to the Bureau of Genetic Welfare and protect the people in the Chicago experiment from mass-erasure. Her ability to resist the medical control used by the power-holders in her world creates a second-hand experience for young readers, allowing them the opportunity to see and imagine a situation where they can refuse to be medicated for their divergence. It portrays the resistance of these oppressive methods in a very positive light. Without Tris's serum resistance, the Bureau would've reset the population of Chicago; destroying the personalities of thousands of people in the process.

While the mass-drugging of youth is often considered damaging—both physically and mentally—to a young person, as the publication *Consumer Reports* points out, there are some young people who take ADHD medication and report a positive change in their behavior. Some youth want to change, and the medication allows them to take an active role in their personal development; allowing them to exercise some power and control over their situation. This allows them to exercise external control—medication—in order to develop their internal control. When a person genuinely believes that their behavior is incorrect, but can't seem to change, then medication can offer them a tangible method of improvement. If they choose to take it, then it becomes a method of personal control.

Occasionally, a character in *Divergent* will choose to take serum because it gives them control over a situation. Peter, for example, uses the serum after he becomes unhappy with his own behavior. He doesn't know how to change, so he takes the memory serum in the hopes that it will give him some control over the situation: "He is afraid that he will not be able to put in that work, that he will squander those days, and that they will leave him worse off than he is now." The memory serum gives Peter the power to change who he is, and—crucially—it's his *choice* to take it. Likewise, Tobias frequently injects himself with fear serum to confront the things which frighten him. While the fear serum is mainly used to terrorize new initiates, Tobias takes control of the serum by *choosing* how often he wants to experience his worst fears. These characters exercise control in the face of a regime which requires their obedience to a set of personality traits by choosing when, and how, they are exposed to the serums.

Fear and Hope for the Future

Unfortunately, there's little information available about the long-term effects of ADHD medication because the generation most affected by it is still in adolescence. It will be many years before we learn whether we've irretrievably damaged the youth of today in the hopes of making them "better," or whether our fears are unfounded. Stories like *Divergent*, which deal directly with the medical control of youth, paint a very disturbing picture of a world where divergence from the norm is so dangerous that it must be medically corrected. But they also offer hope. Characters like Peter and Tobias take control of their lives by appropriating the serums for their own purposes, and Tris's ability to outright reject the control of serums offers the reader a vicarious experience of power in the face of overwhelming control.

2
Peculiar!

CHRISTOPHER KETCHAM

At the end of Veronica Roth's second book of the *Divergent* series, *Insurgent*, and then in the third book, *Allegiant*, we discover that the factions are an experiment to correct a disastrous foray into eugenics—the "science" of improving the quality of humans through selective genetics and breeding.

The original goal of this genetic experimentation was to modify human genetic traits deemed undesirable in society. However, the genetically modified people were considered cognitively damaged because they could only exhibit one desired trait. The Purity War began when the genetically damaged rose up against the genetically pure, and the government in general. The war produced the apocalyptic destruction of civilization and society, the aftermath of which is still being felt at the time of the *Divergent* stories.

After this disastrous war, the Bureau of Genetic Welfare tried to reverse the genetic damage. One corrective attempt is the Chicago experiment, which segregates individuals into behaviorally distinct factions with faction-specific serums and psycho-modification strategies designed to make them productive members of society, but in different and segregated factions. The rationale is that since nothing can be done about people's genes, the people can be segregated into programmed behavioral modification routines that will eliminate the unwanted behaviors that result from their defective genes. So each faction is different from the other because each faction features a particular genetic defect that others presumably don't have. There's also a serum that identifies the defect, which points individuals towards *the* faction that can help mitigate the effects of the bad gene. But there are some who fall through the cracks and never pass the initiation rites to join a faction, or who fail to qualify for only one faction—the Divergent. Those who fail the initiation are thrown down into the bottomless pit of existence called "factionless," with no way out . . . until . . .

The Bureau believes the experiment must continue—at any cost. Their plan is to turn back the efforts of the factionless, who are trying to lift themselves from poverty and despair, by erasing the memory of every Chicagoan and restarting the experiment. For the Bureau, the experiment is more important than the needs of the people. Ridiculous you say? Not possible in the real Chicago or anywhere in the real United States. Unbelievable? Pure science fiction?

Tuskegee Experiment

In 1932 the US Public Health Service—now Centers for Disease Control (CDC)—began working with the Tuskegee Institute, founded by Booker T. Washington (1856–1915), to study syphilis in six-hundred poor, mostly uneducated black men who didn't have the means or the intention to leave Macon County, Alabama—they were factionless! Some had syphilis and some did not. For participating in the study the men received free medical exams, free meals, and burial insurance.

None of the participants gave his informed consent. In other words, they weren't told why the group was being studied and what it was being studied for. Nor were they informed about any personal consequences, health or otherwise they could or would face. All were told that they were being treated for "bad blood," but the truth is, no one received any medical care for syphilis, not even after a treatment became widely available in 1947. In fact, local physicians were told not to treat the men for syphilis. The study was supposed to last for six months, but dragged on under its own bureaucratic weight, until 1936 when the study leaders—think, the Bureau—decided to follow the men until they died, never treating anyone with syphilis.

Syphilis is a long, agonizing, and debilitating disease that can, in its tertiary stage, lead to dementia and ultimately death. Even as late as 1969 the CDC and local AMA (American

Medical Association) chapters vowed to continue the study without treating any participant. However, some doctors ignored the moratorium and treated these men, and as a result, many of these doctors were admonished by authorities for their transgression. The study ended in 1972 when the Associated Press broke the story about the experiment. Even after being discredited, some researchers still defended the soundness of the study and its methods into the 1980s. Can't happen here? Did happen here, and you can get more details at: http://www.cdc.gov/tuskegee/timeline.htm.

The Beginnings of Peculiar

For the people of Chicago it goes deeper than informed consent. They don't know they're in an experiment until the end of *Insurgent*, when Edith Prior (Amanda Ritter), a Bureau plant, explains so on a video. This is a shock, but the factions and the factionless alike have always known that they are peculiar. The Chicagoans either belong to different groups called factions or they're factionless—where their service to society, their dress, and their attitude are based upon their genetic anomalies— their peculiarities. So, what's it like to be peculiar?

Well, it's like being both different and strange at the same time. Different, meaning my leather jacket is different from your sport coat; and strange, well, this difference unnerves you perhaps to the point where you want to cross the street to avoid me. So, *who* is peculiar? It's anyone who's different, different enough to be peculiar! Well that's just the kind of circular logic that'll get you excoriated, eviscerated, and expunged from the Philosopher's Union.

But listen. Peculiar is in the mind of the beholder, right? When you were growing up weren't you told not to go near "those people" because there's something untoward—peculiar—about them? "They're all drunks; they live like pigs— every house needs a coat of paint; they're all crooks—why they'll eat your lunch; they sleep around and they all live in broken homes where the fathers have run off. They aren't like us, so keep your distance." By proxy, of course, they are the peculiars—the Amity, Candor, Erudite, Abnegation, and Dauntless or Divergent . . . whoever you aren't. Truthfully, they're all peculiar to each other, "Like, who would want to be one of *them*. Girl, seriously, gag me with a spoon before that!"

But hey, aren't we all mutants in some way, and as a result, a little bit peculiar to someone else? What is it about this Chicago experiment that has the people in disarray over whether factions are good or bad for people? Could it be that while we want to be part of something that is like us, there's still the nagging idea that these peculiar others are people too? And wait, my brother chose Erudite and I Dauntless, but we both grew up in Abnegation—so how's he suddenly so peculiar to me? I know he's a brainiac, but there are smart people in all the factions. Then there are the factionless, but many of them were serum-qualified for a faction but flunked out. Does that mean they should be abandoned to factionless hell? And Divergents are dangerous. But why dangerous?

Think back to Tuskegee—the experimenters wanted the study to continue at *all* costs. In *Allegiant*, the Bureau wants to continue the faction experiment and will do *anything*, even erase the citizens of Chicago's minds to rebuild the experiment after the factionless outlaw factions. Is it really about genetic purity any more, or is it about power, control, and a kind of self-righteousness that comes from being in charge of a massive experiment? So, how did we get here—this *Divergent* place where people are categorized and segregated into lifestyles, behavioral routines, and jobs that they truly cannot aspire to escape from?

First, it isn't about race or ethnicity. For factions, it's about how you think, or better yet, how your genes *require* you to think. With a simple aptitude test we can tell you the faction where you should belong. But unlike the racial purity tests of the Nazis and American segregation, it doesn't matter who your parents or grandparents are—at least not directly. What matters is what your genetic code programs you to be.

By definition your genes make you peculiar, but you don't know until you're a teenager which type of peculiar you actually are—in other words, which faction you "should" join to be conditioned to conform to their unique culture and practices. And if you discover you're Divergent, you're dangerous! Don't divulge it, and be very scared that your faction will root you out, which means becoming factionless for sure, and possibly even lead to your death. And why should this be so—remember, what the Bureau wants, the Bureau gets.

Factions have become the ruling classes, even if it's the case that the factions were originally intended to be correctional groups that could work together in harmony in different societal roles. In theory the factions are behavioral clinics to function only until the time they become unnecessary, when enough genetically pure individuals are born. The Bureau knows that the resurgence of genetic purity is already happening because of the increase of Divergent citizens. But the experiment must continue! And the factionless, well they're considered expendable, just as a few hundred black men from Alabama were considered expendable.

How Can I Relate to Factions?

I have a hard time relating to these factions, you say. We have nothing like that in my town. So, help me understand. Think about it, are factions really any different from what we voluntarily subject ourselves to today? What about joining a local gang, or the military, or even going to college? Don't they all have gatekeepers to protect the gang, army, and school from those who will not fit the mold? Don't they all brainwash you? Don't they all require you to conform to their culture and practices? Don't they all call for you to go through ritual initiation rites to be considered gangbanger, private first class, or degree holder? Tell me then, what's the difference?

Maybe not much. In America you take the SAT or ACT, which when combined with your grades, tells you what tier college you can reasonably expect to apply to. Let's put a *Divergent* twist on this: what if someone develops a serum that tells you which vocation, school or gang you have aptitude for and which the authorities say is foolproof? But then there's a catch—if you don't take the serum you'll be put where the others who flunk out go. Wouldn't you take the serum and make the best of it? You take the test now and are relegated to the schools and careers it says you're qualified for. And, sure, if you don't work hard you flunk out and do the menial jobs that nobody else wants.

It isn't exactly the same because in the post-Purity War world of *Divergent*, it isn't how smart you are but what your genetic damage is that needs to be corrected by behavior modification. In *Divergent*, "Big Brother Gene" is watching you. For us it's "Big Brother Test."

If you fail to become a member of the faction that the serum test chooses for you; well, you can always become factionless. But where does that get you? Factionless is the fate of failure, the fall into meaninglessness, because there's no way out, no way back into a faction. At least in the world of the SAT and ACT, even if you flunk out or find that menial jobs aren't your thing, we say, "You can bite and claw your way back to school, or learn the skills that will get you a better-paying, more rewarding job." But why are there still poor people in our society who live like the factionless in *Divergent*—don't they know they can get out? Or can they? Is there a built in prejudice against them, like the prejudice against the *Divergent* factionless that helps to keep the poor where they are?

Racial IQ and Culture

Sometimes the tests don't give us good answers, or worse the wrong answers which can lead to dire consequences. The early IQ tests were formulated by people who were part of the white culture of the Eastern United States in the early twentieth century. As a result, many of the words and pictures were unfamiliar, or had different meanings to some of the test takers, especially for non-whites. Also, Northern African Americans scored differently from Southern African Americans. Researchers like Otto Klineberg explained this phenomenon with the disgraced theory that "better" black people migrated north, which appeared in the 1934 *Journal of Negro Education*'s issue dedicated to examining theories of race psychology and testing. Even today, some studies like Richard Herrnstein and Charles Murray's *The Bell Curve*, and Sowell's *Intellectuals and Race*, attempt to tie intelligence to race. So the implications are that if some races are less intelligent, they should not be given the jobs that require intelligence . . . relegating them to jobs that generally pay less.

Against such conclusions, there have also been many well researched articles that explain that IQ differences have *nothing* to do with race, but instead, can be explained by cultural differences. Say you come from a rural culture that has no experience with an inkwell or an Edsel car, how could you possibly answer the questions the IQ test asks about these correctly? You just guess and likely get it wrong, and this brands you and others like you from your culture as below average. People get branded quickly. Consider that those who were in charge of the Tuskegee experiment believed they were dealing with small-brained over-sexed animals. Wait, that's just plain prejudice! I guess they didn't get the memo.

We continue to wrestle with the problem of racial stereotypes today, both in society and in IQ and other assessments. But race isn't the problem in the *Divergent* series. For the people of Chicago, the Bureau determines what's normal based on *their* cultural biases. As a result, cultural tensions based on these biases result. People test for specific factions, but fail to meet the qualifications to become members. There are those like Tris who qualify for more than one faction. People are taught that it's in their best interest to join the faction suggested by the serum, but they don't have to. Even more unnerving is the fact that if you can't make the cut, you can't transfer to a faction that might actually cure your genetic behavioral anomaly. Doesn't add up, right? There's something besides genes at work here, and it's the cultural meddling of the Bureau. They want us to be different and strange and feel different and strange. But that's just peculiar, isn't it? True, but there are psychological implications of feeling peculiar.

I Get the Feeling I Don't Belong

The early twentieth-century educator and civil rights advocate, W.E.B. Dubois (1868–1963), in his book *The Souls of Black Folk*, explained that early in elementary school another child refused to have anything to do with him. As a result, Dubois began to see that he didn't belong. He called it his "twoness": being both black and American, a dual consciousness for which he felt alienated, sometimes by both groups. He was black, but he didn't fit the stereotypical black person, as understood by whites. He was American, but black people were legally segregated from whites in many parts of the country, and in other areas, many just didn't mingle with whites. Dubois saw that "separate but equal" was "separate but not at all equal."

Dubois was peculiar. Tris is peculiar. Four (Tobias) is peculiar. The factions are peculiar to each other. Dubois was born in Massachusetts—a non-segregation state, was intelligent and eloquent, and the first African American to earn a doctorate at

Harvard. Tris was born into Abnegation, thrives in Dauntless, but underneath it all she's Divergent—her "twoness" is that while she thrives in Dauntless she really doesn't belong in any faction! Remember there is no behavioral-modification faction called Divergent . . . you're on your own. Her intelligence is that she has a well-honed intuition about people, politics, and battle. Four is also smart and capable, and believes that he's Divergent; though later tests reveal he isn't: his "twoness". What drives it all are the biased beliefs of the Bureau about genes and what's normal.

Like Tuskegee, things simply have gotten out of control in the world of *Divergent*. The stereotypes remain at the forefront of those who are in power at the Bureau, regardless of the evidence that the people from Chicago don't fit their expected mold. Tobias seems as Divergent as the rest, though he failed to "test" *genetically* Divergent. Think back to Dubois. How did he feel when his classmate shunned him? Like his world had been pulled out from under him. The world of Tobias pulled out from under him when he finds out he isn't Divergent; he's only Dauntless, just another category of difference . . . peculiar. The power of discrimination, racial stereotyping, genotyping, and other forms of oppression and segregation as Dubois discovered and Tobias is learning is that once one is labeled "peculiar" by society it's difficult, if not impossible to change that moniker.

A Lesser Evil

Is there a cure to the "syphilis" of *Divergent*? Is the cure the status quo, as was the path at Tuskegee? Is it to erase the minds of Chicagoans and restart the factions? Is it to erase the minds of the Bureau people to reset the experiment back to zero, in order to remove genetic discrimination from the experimental controllers' memory? *Allegiant* takes the last option.

Wouldn't it be nice if we had a serum like that which could cure intractable discrimination in the US and in many other parts of the world by erasing it from the mind? Of course, this isn't possible, and eradicating someone's memory is certainly not something you'll find in most ethics playbooks. Roth's solution leaves a major problem: the residents of Chicago still have the memories of factions: the visible scars, the learned behaviors, the clothes, old tensions, which will lead to new ones, and who knows what the legacy of genetic tampering will produce?

Because the residents have bought into the faction system for so long, the narrative of the faction system will work to keep the oppressed peoples of Chicago oppressed. The renowned Marxist thinker Antonio Gramsci (as expounded by Kate Crehan) showed that the oppressed have their own hierarchies of action and response, so it's difficult for the oppressed to break out of oppression because they have, in some respects, bought into the story that the oppressor told about how things are and ought to be. Roth's Chicagoans have bought into factions, genetically pure, and genetically damaged and what all these mean. So while their ultimate oppressor, the Bureau, at the end of *Allegiant* has no memory of these things, the people do.

Gramsci would propose that someone needs to leave the faction, learn what the world outside is like, and return as an "organic intellectual," in order to teach them how best to live. This is not unlike Plato's analogy of the cave, where one prisoner escapes the cave of shadows, enters the outside world of true knowledge, and then returns to the cave to educate the remaining prisoners.

Who will be Gramsci's organic intellectuals, who help those who have been subjects of the grand experiment gone wrong understand the world without the controlling influence of factions or the Bureau? Will it be Tobias, Johanna, Evelyn, or even Zeke, Christina, Shauna or Matthew? Regardless of who it is, there needs to be a replacement for factions developed by someone besides those inculcated by the Bureau. Perhaps that's where Veronica Roth wants to leave us, thinking for ourselves and aware of our surroundings and of the inevitable hegemony that results from any bureaucracy that's allowed to exist and perform "experiments" without oversight, control, or recourse.

Here's an idea: perhaps the answer is praxis. Paulo Freire, the great educator of the oppressed in the slums of South America, defined praxis in his book *Pedagogy of the Oppressed* as: "reflection and action upon the world in order to transform it." If the *Divergent* series is a critique of our own society then the continuation of the story could use some praxis. As the mutants reflect upon what government has done to create their anomalies and the disastrous experiment to correct them, what kind of transformation will they build to re-enter the human race? And can they, as we have yet been unable to do with years of civil rights struggles, constitutional amendments, laws, and seemingly endless discourse about equality, discover a place where people are just people and not peculiars?

We can't just ask Veronica Roth to go out and write this for us. We need to write the continuation, to be the organic intellectuals, to engage in the praxis necessary to eliminate factions in our own society. And what would you call this continuation? Why not Justice?

3
Tris Finds Enlightenment

MARJORIE E. RHINE

What good is a prepared body if you have a scattered mind?

—TRIS

One thing that you probably notice right away when reading *Divergent* is that it's a story set in the future. This future has its problems, you soon see, and if you've read similar young adult novels set in a bleak future, you know what to expect: the young hero will challenge and defeat the corrupt system.

This turns out to be true. The young hero, Beatrice—who soon shortens her name to Tris—has unique skills due to her multifaceted, Divergent mind. Most people in her society fit into one of five factions, social groups that share similar values and lifestyles and whose members respond to the world with similar strategies. Tris, however, combines several of these strategies, and she uses them to assess new information and events and to come up with approaches to solving problems from multiple points of view. She's able to understand key information and act on it decisively, in a way that makes her a natural leader. She's quick to grasp the essentials of the developing crisis, and she sees the truth of a situation when others don't. For instance, before anyone else, she sees the serum-induced mental simulations, used by her society's leaders to induce fear for testing purposes, *as* simulations. Her skills would no doubt make her an astute business leader, as online articles like "5 Business Lessons from the Hit Film Divergent" attest.

These skills are tied to her Abnegation upbringing, which grounds her Divergence. What's most interesting, for our purposes, is that they're also closely aligned with practices central to a Buddhist lifestyle and set of beliefs. Tris's heroism depends on several key Buddhist practices, including her ability to closely read others, which is tied to her highly attuned emotional intelligence, and her use of calming meditative techniques, such as an attention to breathing and a total focus on the present. What's more, as current neuroscience research reveals, these practices also align with brain activity that allows us to better control irrational fears and heighten problem-solving. So, let's see how Abnegation and Tris's abilities correspond to Buddhism and contemporary neuroscience.

Our Hero's World

The five factions that structure Tris's society were designed to be an effective way of organizing social life to prevent a repeat of the war that devastated Chicago. Late in the series, readers learn that the five factions were created as a social engineering experiment to inspire Divergence to arise—a trait recognized as valuable to human society after leaders in the past had tried to eradicate it. However, in the first novel, we don't yet know this. We take the factions at face value, assuming that they're intended to promote peace.

Early in *Divergent*, we learn tidbits of information about these factions as Tris, telling her story, introduces us to her world. We see Tris's unease with the self-denial Abnegation requires, in the opening scene as her mother cuts her hair. We see the Candor man on the bus and learn that this faction values complete honesty. We see Erudite students chattering over books and newspapers, and Dauntless members fearlessly leaping from a moving train. We see Amity teenagers playing a hand-slapping game and laughing as they wait for their aptitude test. In addition, when Tris encounters a factionless man, we see how these outcasts live and how scary they are to the rest of society.

After these initial glimpses of the factions, you might be wondering how this society became organized in this unusual way. This is explained at the Choosing Ceremony. As Marcus Eaton explains:

> Decades ago our ancestors realized that it is not political ideology, religions, belief, race, or nationalism that is to blame for a warring

world. Rather, they determined that it was the fault of human personality—of humankind's inclination toward evil, in whatever form that is. They divided into factions that sought to eradicate those qualities they believed responsible for the world's disarray.

People who blamed human evil on aggression formed Amity. Those who saw ignorance as the root of evil became the Erudite. People who believed duplicity was the root of conflict created Candor. Those who understood selfishness as the source of human troubles formed the Abnegation faction. Those who saw evil's source in cowardice became Dauntless. Abnegation provides selfless leaders, Candor provides lawyers and judges, Erudite supplies teachers and researchers, Amity provides counselors and caretakers, and Dauntless provides protection.

The society Marcus describes is one that places a high value on order and, ideally, functions like an organism whose parts all serve a clear function and work together for society's maximum effectiveness, which resembles the sociological theory known as "structural functionalism." In this "organism," faction members are expected to perform the social roles that their respective faction dictates. Shared faction norms are so important that their overriding motto is "Faction Before Blood."

However, the supposedly smooth functioning of the society that Marcus celebrates at the Choosing Ceremony is not reality. Rumors accuse Abnegation of hogging goods and foods for themselves, and these rumors create hostility between different factions, which culminates in a war between Erudite and Abnegation factions, with mind-altered Dauntless used as soldiers.

Diminishing the Ego

Tris's Abnegation upbringing influences her later success, but Tris's unique brand of Abnegation practices seem rooted in Buddhist traditions. Most obviously, self-abnegation is a term often associated with Buddhism. According to basic histories of Buddhism, which you can easily find at websites like asiasociety.org, Buddhism was founded in the late sixth century B.C.E. by Siddhartha Gautama—born about 563 B.C.E., in the Himalayan foothills. Siddhartha grew up as a Hindu prince in a time of spiritual, intellectual, and social ferment. He eventually rejected the luxuries of his princely life, in order to seek a spiritual response adequate for the very real human suffering he witnessed as a young man—despite his father's efforts to shield him from such sights.

During his spiritual journey, and eventual enlightenment, Siddhartha became the Buddha—or awakened one—and turned away from traditional Hindu emphases on ritual. He also rejected the extreme self-abnegation of the Jainists, another religious group emerging around the same time. According to Puqun Li, Jainist belief centers on freeing the soul by overcoming instincts that arise from the physical body. Severe austere practices, such as restricting food intake, are intended to weaken the physical body, which is supposed to then motivate the soul's release from the body.

Since Buddhism rejects extreme self-abnegation—often called asceticism—the central tenets of Buddhism do not support the strict self-abnegation people sometimes associate with Buddhist nuns and monks. Instead, Buddhism supports a "middle way" that "diverges" from extreme asceticism and extreme pleasures.

Buddhism's central message is both devastatingly simple, yet mind-bogglingly complex: life is suffering (*dukkha*). We suffer from trying to cling to things we enjoy or love, fearful that our joys or loves will end or die. So, suffering—our unease, our anxieties—is caused by clinging or craving to things in this life. In his example and teachings, Buddha offers a way out: we can end suffering by following an "Eightfold Path," guidelines that help us structure our lives in ways that decrease the needy, clinging demands of the ego.

According to Buddhism, most of us wrongly identify with the voice in our head—our stream of thoughts—and identify this voice as "Me." We fight to protect this "me" (or ego), struggling to prove that we are right, complaining about others to enhance our own superiority, and getting defensive and aggressive to prove ourselves right. This is how we fortify our sense of self.

Eckhart Tolle offers some useful descriptions of this kind of ego-posturing in his book *The New Earth*. The defense of our ego often plays out in ridiculous but potentially dangerous ways, such as when we try to prove that we were wronged, or try to get revenge for a perceived wrongdoing—like in a road rage conflict. The person who cut us off on the highway may be merely hurrying to pick up a sick child from school, but our emotions kick in quickly and prevent us from seeing reality from an objective viewpoint. Instead, we take the offense as something personal, and we try to protect and defend our own unenlightened sense of self. This, according to Buddhist thought, is the root of all suffering and conflict.

Tris remembers her father's wisdom about how hunger for power creates people who cling to fantasies of power and aggressively work to maintain it: "My father says that those who want power and get it live in terror of losing it. That's why we have to give power to those who do not want it." The self-denial of Abnegation is focused on working to calm the ego's greedy hunger for prominence, an antidote to conflict.

The calming of the ego is also seen in Abnegation neighborhoods and houses. As Tris explains in *Divergent*:

> The houses on my street are all the same size and shape. They are made of gray cement, with few windows, in economical, no-nonsense rectangles. Their lawns are crabgrass and their mailboxes are dull metal. To some the sight might be gloomy, but to me their simplicity is comforting. The reason for the simplicity isn't disdain for uniqueness, as the other factions have sometimes interpreted it. Everything—our houses, our clothes—our hairstyles—is meant to help us forget ourselves and to protect us from vanity, greed and envy, which are just forms of selfishness. If we have little, and want for little, and we are all equal, we envy no one.

Yes, everything is meant to help them forget themselves, to ease the greedy hunger of the ego. They renounce the vanity of admiring their looks in a mirror. They wear dull grey clothes that downplay beauty, and they cultivate a ready selflessness that compels them to give up their seat on the bus to others. They've learned to sit quietly when they have to wait, rather than playing games, acting rowdy, or arguing. They're modest, unaccustomed to revealing their bodies, and they eat plain, simple food. Tris has never had a hamburger until she becomes Dauntless!

However, the extreme self-denial in Abnegation is a bit different than the goals of Buddhist practice. The story of the Buddha's discovery of the path to enlightenment stresses the importance of following a "middle way": enjoy life's simple pleasures, but don't cling to them obsessively. Thus, in a Buddhist sense, Tris is right to question the extreme self-denial that characterizes the lifestyle in Abnegation, but she's also right to practice her moderate self-denial when everyone else clings to excess. These character traits serve her well in her future pursuits.

Tris's Buddhist Traits

Tris practices several Abnegation strategies when confronted by challenges that although not uniquely Buddhist are indeed associated with Buddhist practice. Early on in her Dauntless training, she appears well-versed in using awareness of the breath to control her fears. When she slips while descending the Ferris wheel at Navy Pier, she reminds herself as she hangs precariously: "I breathe in my nose and out my mouth. I count my breaths to calm down. One, two. In, out." Counting breaths is a classic way to focus in Buddhist meditation, similar to the meditation practices in yoga classes. If we can get our mind to concentrate on the breath, instead of investing in and following worrisome thoughts flitting through our heads, we can calm down and focus. She uses the same sort of breathing techniques when she helps Four navigate his fear landscape. Since she seems comfortably familiar with this practice, we can assume she practiced it growing up as an Abnegation.

Tris is also skilled at another trait typically enhanced by Buddhist practice: "reading" what's going on with other people. This skill shows her "emotional intelligence," defined in the well-known book of that title by Daniel Goleman, as the ability to perceive, reason from, and respond to the emotions of others. Because of this skill, she astutely observes subtle power relationships, like when Four and Eric interact. She naturally senses the discord and tension between them. Her ability to read these emotional messages, which helps her navigate her way to success, is probably linked to the Abnegation practice of putting other people's needs before her own, which requires perceptively assessing the needs of others by paying close attention to their emotions.

A third Buddhist practice Tris exhibits is the ability to be aware of the voices in her head. She's conscious of these voices, which helps her avoid simply succumbing to the conditioning of her past. This awareness, and ability to control it, is one of the main goals of the practice of Buddhist meditation. To some extent, she has to overcome lessons instilled by her parents to become successful as Dauntless. She does more than simply remember the life lessons taught to her as an Abnegation child; she's hyper-aware of them *as* actual voices in her head. She doesn't let them unconsciously shape her response. Instead, she articulates the lesson, assesses it, and determines whether or not the lesson is relevant in the context of the problem she faces. During the climactic fight with Molly, she tells us, "My mother and father would not approve of my kicking someone when she's down. I don't care." Although she arguably succumbs to strong emotions in this scene, in a way she usually avoids, her ability to be aware of and yet distinct from the thoughts that flash through her mind is a desirable skill sought after in Buddhist practice.

Divergent Brain Science and Buddhism

As Tris learns in conversations with both her mother and with Jeanine, most people who are Divergent arise from within the Abnegation faction. Why might this be? Perhaps, as I suggested above, the constant practice of putting others' needs before one's own strengthens the ability of the brain to control an overly emotional, reactive response. When this happens, the part of our brain associated with reason and forethought, the prefrontal cortex, plays a larger part in controlling what might arise as selfish emotions. As discussed in works by Andrea Grabovac and Richard J. Davidson, neuroscientists have provided evidence—with the help of functional MRIs—that after training in meditation, the prefrontal cortex becomes more active; it more easily controls the activity of the amygdala, a region of the brain commonly associated with fear.

This explanation from neuroscience is seen in the book when Four explains that the serum of the fear landscape stimulates the amygdala. Will, a young man training as Dauntless who is a transfer from Erudite, also explains to Tris about the science behind the fear simulations. Will says, "It's basically a struggle between your thalamus, which is producing the fear, and your frontal lobe, which makes decisions. But the simulation is all in your head, so even though you feel like someone is doing it to you, it is just you, doing it to yourself."

Although Four refers to the amygdala, whereas Will refers to the thalamus, both of these brain structures are part of the brain's limbic system, which processes fears and emotions. Tris remembers Will's words later, and his words help her to overcome her fear during a simulation. Knowing about what's happening in her brain in a lucid, conscious way allows her to recognize that the fear she's facing doesn't originate from an external reality. It's literally all in her mind, just as Buddhists would say all of life's simulations are.

Even though most of us will never experience what the Dauntless initiates do, we often do encounter similar situations. If someone responds to you gruffly or in a tone of voice that triggers past memories that summon fear, you might feel fearful. But perhaps this gruff person is angry or frustrated for other reasons. Maybe you *feel* like someone is doing something to you, but, as Will says, "It is just you, doing it to yourself." It's how you're responding that is creating the fear. If you can learn to become aware of what triggers you to feel this way, this awareness can help you free yourself from this kind of "simulation" more quickly. But cultivating that awareness isn't an easy task: hence, the need for continual meditation and practice.

Tris emerges most clearly as a hero understandable through a Buddhist lens in her ability to see the simulation *as* a simulation, to know so quickly and so clearly that *"The simulation is all in your head."* In this way, she is not unlike Neo in *The Matrix,* who is in the end able to manipulate the rules of the Matrix and thus defeat the agents. As Tori tells Tris, "You are someone who is aware, when they are in a simulation, that what they are experiencing is not real. . . . Someone who can then manipulate the simulation or even shut it down."

This ability stems not only from Tris's Abnegation but also from her being Divergent. Four has much the same background: he was raised as Abnegation and classified as Divergent. Yet Tris, unlike Four, somehow lights up when in danger. Four tells her, "Fear doesn't shut you down; it wakes you up." When she's climbing the Ferris wheel she feels fully, intensively alive: "the height makes me feel alive with energy, every organ and muscle in my body singing at the same pitch." When she focuses on the task of turning off the deadly simulation at the end of the book, she's like an athlete "in the zone," so attuned to the task at hand that thinking is left behind as the body flows into movement: "I have tunnel vision, I am running along this path and I will not be able to stop, will not be able to think of anything, until I reach the end."

Perhaps Tris's multifaceted, Divergent mind allows a top performance not unlike that of Buddhist monks with long meditation experience. As Sharon Begley shows in *Train Your Mind, Change Your Brain*, the brain scans of Buddhist monks show a tremendous increase in gamma activity, a heightened state of the brain associated with perception and problem-solving. Based on data from the website Brain Works—brainworksneurotherapy.com—it's possible that Tris's Divergence is the result of gamma brainwaves simultaneously processing information from different brain areas.

Brain Works also suggests that gamma waves, which connect neurons at a higher frequency than other brain waves, are "the most subtle of the brainwave frequencies," and so, the mind "has to be quiet to access it." Meditation is the best way to "quiet" the mind. Researchers have also discovered that gamma waves are most active when people are in a state of mind linked to the cultivation of compassion, love, or altruism. The need for the mind to be quiet, and the link between gamma waves and altruism, suggest that Abnegation practices may indeed create ideal conditions for individuals to use their minds at peak performance. In other words, learning how to be quiet and observe others' needs first, and cultivating altruism, may lead to an increase in gamma brainwaves, where the brain is firing on all cylinders. In this way, the findings of contemporary neuroscience align with the novel's emphasis that the desired brain trait known as "Divergent" arises most often in the Abnegation faction.

Meditative Thoughts

Looking at Tris's heroism through the lens of Buddhism helps us imagine ways that we could all be more like Tris in our own lives, even though our lives are far different than her fictional one. We all can feel trapped in glass cages at times—struggling as stressful tasks or challenges mount up, or feeling, perhaps, as if we're drowning, unable to stay afloat. But sometimes a slight shift in our understanding or reaction can shatter the glass, or at least start it cracking. As Tris says, "Half of bravery is perspective."

Maybe we can edit our to-do lists to be more like an Abnegation: find a little breathing air and quiet time for our thoughts. Maybe we can practice gratitude and find small things to be thankful for that lift our spirits, lessening our tight focus on self-troubles and self-challenges. Maybe a little more quiet time will allow our minds to become more mobile—agile at moving in different directions, quick at making connections, and good at making decisions. As Tris's mother tells her in what ends up being their last conversation:

> Every faction conditions its members to think and act a certain way. And most people do it. For most people, it's not hard to learn, to find a pattern of thought that works and stay that way. . . . But our minds move in in a dozen different directions. We can't be confined to one way of thinking, and that terrifies our leaders. It means we can't be controlled. And that means that no matter what they do, we will always cause trouble for them.

Let's hope that trouble-makers always arise, challenging oppressive systems that try to control the indomitable human spirit.

4

Nietzsche's Faction Test

LAURA MALLALIEU

Let me declare expressly that in the days when mankind was not yet ashamed of its cruelty, life on earth was more cheerful than it is now that pessimists exist.

—FRIEDRICH NIETZSCHE, *On the Genealogy of Morals*

Human reason can excuse any evil; that is why it's so important that we don't rely on it.

—ANDREW PRIOR, *Divergent*

What could nineteenth-century philosopher Friedrich Nietzsche possibly have to say about Veronica Roth's dystopian *Divergent* series?

Nietzsche proposes an overhaul of current morals, like pity and compassion, while *Divergent* allows us to see what experiments in overhauling values might look like, using new political structures and restrictions on knowledge to create new worlds and imposed value systems. Looking at Nietzsche's ideas of forgetting, the will to power, and the slave rebellion, along with *Divergent*'s faction systems and memory serum, allows us to explore all the moral issues raised by these topics. These issues include whether or not it's possible to promote one value without creating a corresponding vice, what it means to exert your will despite moral restrictions, whether it's justified to use memory loss to improve society, and whether or not we can lose our memories without losing our identities. It also provides a canvas on which to consider hypothetical situations of what Nietzsche's ideas might look like if he were able to implement his own experiment on changing the morals of society.

Getting to Know Nietzsche and *Divergent*

The events recounted in the *Divergent* Series take place in a future Chicago where values and morals are different than they are today. The Chicago where Tris and Tobias, two of the main characters, grow up is created around the idea that the vices of cowardice, selfishness, aggression, ignorance, and falsity create war.

The city is divided up into five different factions with the hope of combating those vices with the values of bravery, selflessness, amiableness, intelligence, and truth. However, this society, and its value system, is an experiment. In the wake of a war between the Genetically Pure (GP) and the Genetically Damaged (GD), the US government used polluted genetics as reasoning to justify a series of genetic experiments on the population.

The government has access to a memory serum that allows them to create people who are completely blank slates and organize them in new isolated political structures based on a created value system. They do this by withholding all information about the past, forming a new city, and setting up the structure of the five factions. The Bureau of Genetic Welfare's artificially constructed value system creates a whole host of problems for the inhabitants of Chicago. They must fight, ally themselves, pledge themselves, and in Tris's case give her life in order to create a better world based on authentically chosen values.

In Nietzsche's essays *Human, All Too Human*, *The Dawn*, *Beyond Good and Evil*, and *On the Genealogy of Morals*, he explains the concept that unlike the ancient Greeks and Romans, Western society is ruled by a slave morality which makes the strong feel guilty for dominating the weak and exerting their power. He maintains that we should eliminate this slave morality and create a new system by which to organize our values, a master morality.

Nietzsche suggests that this new structure should be based on the basic human impulse to exert control over one's will and to operate freely, which he refers to as the "will to power." This new system would operate based on good and bad consequences of actions instead of good or evil intentions and would come about as a part of rejecting and forgetting the old system of morals, which currently equates success and self-promotion with evil and sin. Nietzsche believes that strong people should be free of the guilt of slave morality and able to exercise their own will. The people living and exerting themselves under this new system of morals are referred to as the *Übermensch* (over-man or super-man). Nietzsche himself doesn't claim to be an *Übermensch*, since he grew up with and is still influenced by the slave morality of guilt, but he desires a world in which the *Übermensch* can exist.

Enforcing Alternative Morals

Both Nietzsche and the *Divergent* series envision the creation of a new value system and way of living because they believe that the current society has problems which can be changed by establishing new morals. In Nietzsche's opinion these problems are guilt and self-denial, and in the *Divergent* series they are war and chaos.

In the *Divergent* series, the factions system is created as the way to fix those problems. Each faction is thus organized around a different binary idea of what society should value and what the main problem is in society. These factions are: Dauntless, Abnegation, Erudite, Candor, and Amity. Dauntless seeks to overcome cowardice by valuing bravery, Abnegation to overcome selfishness through selflessness, Erudite to overcome ignorance with knowledge, Candor to overcome dishonesty with honesty, and Amity to overcome violence with peace.

Much like these man-made moral groups, Nietzsche's idea can also be broken down into a binary problem-solution formula. Nietzsche argues that the societal flaw which we must overcome is self-denial, replacing it with the quality of being self-affirming. This can be seen in his claim that:

> The ripest fruit is the sovereign individual, like only to himself, liberated again from morality of custom, autonomous and supramoral . . . and in him a proud consciousness . . . a consciousness of his own power and freedom, a sensation of mankind come to completion. (*Basic Writings*, 28)

Nietzsche believes that humans should liberate themselves from morals that deny the self, in order to better achieve that power and freedom. The promotion of self-affirmation is thereby paired with the destruction of self-denial.

However, looking at the *Divergent* series alongside Nietzsche can help us realize that the promotion of one virtue or quality to the exclusion of other virtues or qualities can have negative side effects. In the *Divergent* series, though each faction denies one vice in order to promote one virtue, there's always a negative consequence. As Andrew Prior says, in the Erudite faction, "Valuing knowledge above all else results in a lust for power, and that leads men into dark and empty places." In Amity, a desire for peace over violence leads to inaction in the face of injustice, and so on. For the main character Tris, though she loves the simple ways of the Abnegation faction that she grew up in, she finds the selflessness they impose distasteful, since it often turns into a kind of enforced self-denial.

The unfortunate side-effect trend of the promotion of one value leading to other vices can apply to Nietzsche's ideas as well. By creating a society of life-affirming people who do not deny themselves anything, it might lead to the problem of excessive cruelty and domination of the strong over the weak. When a person imposes his own will, he runs the risk of treading over others to achieve it. When speaking about the idealized self-affirming *Übermensch*, Nietzsche poses the question: "This emancipated individual . . . how should he not be aware of his superiority over all those who lack the right to make promises?" It's exactly this attitude of superiority over others that will lead to cruelty, violence, and subjugation in society, which is why it makes sense that Nietzsche claims that the *Übermensch* "is bound to reserve a kick for the feeble windbags who promise without the right to do so." The *Übermensch* may have the power and autonomy to make and keep promises and achieve personal success, but at what cost? Nietzsche may not care about the side-effect of cruelty, but it's still worth considering the fact that the cruelty caused by not considering the needs of others or pitying others may create a society which is only good for a select few strong people.

Are You an Übermensch?

Where do Divergent factions and characters fit into Nietzschean ideas of the *Übermensch* versus the slave morality? In the uprising against the Bureau of Genetic Welfare, the Genetically Damaged could be seen as the slaves, rising up against their masters, the Genetically Pure, in order to make them feel bad for exerting their will and repressing them. The violence is necessary because unless the people band together and force their will upon others, they can't gain any influence or make any change. In the Amity faction, where there's no violence but a lot of peace and equality, the people have no real control or influence. They have to mold themselves to agree with others and are literally repressed—with drugs in this case. This lack of control and influence makes them willing slaves.

For this reason the two groups of people that are most like the "slaves" and least like the ideal of Nietzsche's *Übermensch* are the Amity and, of course, the Abnegation. The Abnegation, who live their lives in order to serve others, are controlled through guilt and made to feel as if they're not good enough, if they have any self-serving thoughts or desires. This is very similar to the slave morality Nietzsche speaks of where being self-affirming is viewed as a sin.

Abnegation, though not explicitly tied to a single religious discourse, seems to be very closely modeled around the image of acting like Jesus, who, according to Christian doctrine, served others in the ultimate way by martyring himself for the world. This can be represented by the description of the ceremony for initiation into the Abnegation faction, where the members "wash the initiate's feet. Then they all share a meal, each person serving food to the person on his left," which is clearly a reference to Jesus's last supper where he washed the feet of his disciples and they broke bread together. However, because you repress your own will and desires when selflessly serving others, Abnegation selflessness would be seen by Nietzsche as a kind of slavery, and directly opposed to his idealized *Übermensch*.

Characters who are Divergent, like Tris and Tobias, are more like the *Übermensch* because they live according to their own self-realized morals, not just the morals that society or their faction forces upon them. Both Tris and Tobias are trained in Dauntless not only to be brave, but also to be vicious and to defeat their opponent at any cost; however, they resist those instructions and find the morals that feel true to them.

This can be represented by the fact that they both break the rules by displaying loyalty to more than one faction in the form of their tattoos, because they uphold more than just one value as important. As Tobias puts it in *Divergent*, "I want to be brave, and selfless, *and* smart, *and* honest." They don't let their restrictive society keep them from living according to their own will, and in that way they can be seen as *Übermenschen*.

The *Divergent* series also, perhaps even more directly, deals with Nietzsche's idea of the *Übermensch* in the case of Peter. If the Abnegation can be seen as the faction most closely following slave morality, then Peter can be seen as the most Nietzschean, *Übermensch*-esque character in the *Divergent* series. As Tris puts it, "Maybe there is some abnegation in everyone, even if they don't know it. Well, in everyone but Peter." Peter imposes his will upon others with almost no other moral compass than that of exchanged favors. He always tries to benefit and promote himself, allying himself with whatever side is currently winning or in power, and is often cruel because of this. In *Allegiant*, Tobias says to Peter, "I like to hurt people too. I can make the cruelest choice. The difference is, sometimes I don't, and you always do, and that makes you evil." Because the system of morals they live under tells Peter that he's "evil" for serving himself and being cruel to others, he feels enormous guilt. This guilt is why he decides to wipe his memory. He says, "I want the serum because I'm sick of being this way. I'm sick of doing bad things and liking it and then wondering what's wrong with me. I want it to be over. I want to start again." He wants to forget in order to free himself of the guilt and pain of slave morality—which Nietzsche believes is a good thing. However, instead of becoming a true *Übermensch*, after his memory is wiped and his pain forgotten, he becomes limited, tamed, and assimilated further into the old moral system by society, which hasn't changed its morality.

Memory Loss for Progress

Peter's memory loss calls attention to an intriguing similarity between Nietzsche and the *Divergent* series: the idea that memory loss can be considered a good thing, and perhaps may even be essential for progress. This concept is important to consider because it's controversial, goes against our intuitions, and by looking at the ways it's represented in both works, perhaps the reader may be able to draw conclusions about whether or not Nietzsche would agree that it's moral to use memory loss as a way of ensuring societal progress.

For Nietzsche, this idea is first introduced in his claims about "forgetting" and the necessity of getting rid of the deeply ingrained memories of our past morals in order to create a world with better morals. He believes that memory is connected to pain, and says that:

> Man could never do without blood, torture, and sacrifices when he felt the need to create a memory for himself; the most dreadful sacrifices and pledges . . . —all this has its origin in the instinct that realized that pain is the most powerful aid to mnemonics. (*Basic Writings*, 29)

It's the pain and guilt caused by exerting our will over others that keeps the memory of slave morality alive. He believes that pain or guilt is also our greatest problem, and so for Nietzsche, it is necessary to forget in order to move forward.

In the *Divergent* series, this idea is present in the form of the memory serum, which can completely wipe out a person's memories. Memory serum is used as a way of creating and controlling the populations within the experiments. The experiments, which created communities with completely new values, needed to first erase all memories of previous value systems. This is a highly controversial thing to do, and the morality of taking someone's memories and values is explored at some length in the series. It's frequently portrayed as a kind of necessary evil. The only people who volunteer to join the Bureau's experiments are those who are desperate, because having your memories wiped is equated with a kind of death.

However, despite the questionable morality of wiping memories, even the heroes of the story eventually come to the conclusion that memory loss is necessary to fix corrupt morals—as Tris, Tobias, and their friends decide to wipe the memories of the Bureau of Genetic Welfare in order to save the memories of the people of Chicago. They do this despite the fact that the people in the Bureau haven't consented to having their memories wiped, and fully knowing that those people will completely forget who they are.

It's even worse than when the Bureau originally wiped people's memories for the experiments, because at least that was voluntary. Tris is aware of this and, when deciding to dose the Bureau with memory serum, she claims that "It's not a perfect situation. But when you have to choose between two bad options, you pick the one that saves the people you love and believe in most." In this way, eventually, even the heroic protagonists of the novel, Tris and Tobias decide, like Nietzsche, that it's necessary to wipe out people's memories, previous attitudes, and prejudices in order to make what they believe to be a positive change in the world. Natalie Prior's idea that "Human beings as a whole cannot be good for long before the bad creeps back in and poisons us again" comes into play here, as does the claim that we, as a society, may need at some points to be forcibly fixed by an outside source. The question remains of whether or not this is entirely moral, especially if it's forced on people from an outside source.

Nietzsche's Divergent Experiment

One question we may ask ourselves as we read about memory serum is how Nietzsche would use it if he were able to create his own experimental city using the tools and resources available to the Bureau of Genetic Welfare. It's useful to imagine how Nietzsche's proposals for morality *might* function if actually applied to a society.

In Nietzsche's *Divergent* experiment, there would probably be no factions; instead there would be only one value promoted: self-affirmation, also known as the will to power. Nietzsche would give the memory serum to the strong people, those who exert their will over others and have power, but currently feel guilt over it. He would give them the serum so that they could choose to wipe out their memories and rid themselves of the guilt of slave morality. This coincides with his views on the value of "forgetting" and the pain of memory. Essentially, he would allow the strong in society to thrive and not worry about the weak.

Unfortunately, for most people the Nietzschean experiment would probably be a bad society to live in. Most people today wouldn't want to live in Nietzsche's experiment if they knew exactly what it would entail. One of the main reasons for this is that if strong people are able to do their will, without worrying at all about the weak, then some cruel people will inevitably hurt others in order to benefit themselves. Most people don't want to be hurt by others as those others try to benefit themselves. For the vast majority, Nietzsche's experiment would mean that they are subjugated to the will of the strong, suffering their cruelty and exploitation in a world that doesn't even punish them with guilt for the wrongs that they do to others.

However, this assumes that all the *Übermenschen* are like Peter. It's also possible that in a world where the strong are able to exert their will, strong people like Tris and Tobias would be able to make great change and benefit society as a whole. When Tris came to the decision to use the memory serum on the Bureau of Genetic Welfare, she was acting her will upon others without regard for the will of others; and she was thus able to save many people. This still creates the problem of strong people acting without regard to the will of others, but it does show that it could be used for good instead of evil. However, there's no guarantee of whether or not the *Übermensch* would be more like Tris and Tobias, fighting to make positive changes in the world, or more like Peter, fighting to promote only himself.

On an individual level, forgetting past morality and memories would only really be beneficial to an *Übermensch* like Peter who suffers so much guilt that anything else is preferable. This isn't the case for characters like Tris and Tobias. Though they are also driven to break the current morality and operate outside the bounds of society, in some ways, it's their current sense of morality and guilt that makes them who they are and that benefits them most. Tobias is often driven to impose his will on others and is, in fact, deeply afraid of this tendency, as he believes that like his father, it'll cause him to become cruel. This is why, in his fear landscape, where he's forced to confront all four fears, the greatest fear he must overcome is the fear of looking into the mirror and becoming his father. Tobias says in *Allegiant* that he's mainly afraid "of the threat he posed to my character, to my future, to my identity." Would he benefit from losing that fear and that guilt? From imposing his will like his father and becoming the person he's afraid to be? The simple answer is "No," because it would entirely change the kind of person that he is.

Change in Values = Change in Identity?

It's possible that even for the people whom Nietzsche's experiment would ultimately give more freedom, joining his experiment would still be undesirable. This is because of one of the most important philosophical issues brought up by Nietzsche and by *Divergent*: Can you lose your system of values without also losing your identity?

It may be the case that when you change your deeply held values, it's possible to become a better or stronger person, perhaps even, as Nietzsche claims, the person you *really* are underneath all the artificial morality imposed upon you. However, the fact remains that all that would matter very little, if *you* don't survive as the *same* person. Numerically, you would of course remain the same. However, the qualitative changes to your personal identity, if your memories were gone and your values completely overhauled, may be drastic enough that you couldn't be said to remain the same person. If you wouldn't be the same person after changing your values, then very few people would ever have a reason to do so, since the person they are would cease to exist.

In the *Divergent* series, this issue comes up when discussing why people would ever willingly join the experiments. It becomes apparent that there would only be two reasons to do such a thing: either out of incredible desperation born of destitution—with the hope of benefitting your family's condition or some other such incentive, or because you have seen, done, or felt things in this life which you no longer wish to remember or deal with. In the second case, as can be seen in the example discussed earlier of Peter, the person is essentially saying that they no longer wish to exist as they are.

Unfortunately for those who would desire a drastic change in societal values, it seems as if, unless desperate or depressed, very few people would have a reason to desire a change in their values on such a scale. It's possible to want a better life, but for most people this is only under the condition that their identity remain the same. As Tris puts it, "I would rather be dead than empty." An *Übermensch* may be better than me—though even this is debatable; but if an *Übermensch* would carelessly toss aside the weak to achieve his goals, then perhaps the *Übermensch* is so unlike me that I'd see an *Übermensch* version of myself as a different person. The idea that with the loss of old values, and the imposition of new values, comes a new identity can clearly be seen in the *Divergent* series after people have been administered the memory serum. When describing someone who has had their memory wiped, one of Tobias's friends claims, "The man you knew doesn't exist anymore; he's as good as dead."

The complete loss of identity also creates the moral issue of whether or not it's permissible to erase a person's past values. In a way, erasing a person's memory is like killing them. After it is done, they're no longer there in the same way. Permanently destroying a person's memories, because it destroys their identity, is effectively the same as killing that person. This is why Tris has to justify erasing the Bureau's minds. With her, it was a 'them or my loved ones' rationality. Admittedly, if you were already an *Übermensch* and operating under a different set of morals, then perhaps this would not matter. However, for people considering the morality of memory erasure today, and under our current system of morals, the issue remains.

The End

By looking at Nietzsche's philosophical work and the ideas, inventions, and fictional situations established in the *Divergent* series, we can see that changing values may be equivalent with changing identities in a way that makes such a change undesirable. Nietzsche's version of how society should be, if played out to its full implications, would create a world that would be good for few people, bad for many people, and would rely on entirely erasing previous morals; thus erasing previous identities.

Looking at these two works together—Roth and Nietzsche— is important because it is the job of both fiction and philosophy to make us think of what *could* be, and then see if we can come up with our own conclusions about what *should* be. Personally, I don't want to live in a world of experiments on controlling values or live in an experiment where my values are thrown out in favor of denying myself nothing.

Like Tobias, "I want to be brave, and selfless, *and* smart, *and* honest," and I don't think I need the freedom to be cruel to others in order to be the best possible version of myself.

II

How to
Make Everyone
Less Evil

5
Overcoming Evil with Love

CHAD A. BOGOSIAN

We all want to be loved, for love is the life-blood of human flourishing. From infancy, we regularly express our need for those close to us to care for us. Babies cry when they're hungry, tired, or need changing. With a trusting glance or delicate reach, they communicate their utter dependence on parents and caregivers. Without parental *affection* children are unable to develop or thrive. As such, being affectionate towards the young is a great gift. But affection is hardly a need of children alone.

Adults need the affection of coaches, teachers, mentors, and friends. Each of these persons enriches our lives in different ways and helps us become uniquely ourselves. Take friends or companions for example. Through shared life interests, friends journey together, and, along the way, they challenge and sharpen each other. As the Ancient Greek philosopher Aristotle argues in his *Nicomachean Ethics*, friendship is essential to the development of the virtues and leading the good life.

Unfortunately, not everyone receives the love they need to flourish. Children are routinely left to themselves or abandoned. Adults go through life with no deep friendships, or they fail to experience affection from those closest to them. Worse yet, those who we think are supposed to love us sometimes hate us. Perhaps they do us great harm, sometimes even intentionally. The net impact here extends to our work, friendships, and every social sphere.

Consider the relationship between Four and his father. His dad's physical abuse might explain why he's unable to get close to others, or why he's afraid to take the main leadership position, or why he has to think twice about helping his dad onto the train towards the end of the movie. Naturally we look for hope and help somewhere. Perhaps we look for it in a serum, a group of friends, or something long-term.

Perhaps there's a good system that can guard against relational harms and ensure human flourishing. What are we willing to sacrifice for such a system? Will the system do any better for us than we can do for ourselves? What are the roots of these relational evils, and how are they best overcome? The movie *Divergent* suggests that evil arises both from a range of systemic and individual vices, while a range of virtues, the chief of which is love, best counteracts these.

Factions, Freedom, and Flourishing

Human history is littered with attempts to craft a socio-political system that will best advance human freedom and flourishing. The film *Divergent* reveals early on that the core intention behind the creation of the faction system was to "reduce conflict and create lasting peace." Who wouldn't want to live in a society like that? What better way to order society than to place people in groups based on their virtue of strength: knowledge, honesty, service, selflessness, or bravery? The answers to these questions will depend in part on whether each of these virtues is sufficient to promote human freedom and flourishing when put in motion with the other four. To see that the five virtues, along with the system, are insufficient, consider what happens to human freedom in the faction system.

Nearly everyone values freedom in two senses: moral and political. We want to believe that we make *morally significant choices* that contribute to our relationships, vocations, and the world. We want to be free to create, inquire, and to discover who we really are. If we have good reason to think that we are subject to manipulation or mind control, then we tend to question whether we are really free. Tris expresses this line of thought when she and her brother encounter Jeanine at the faction Choosing Ceremony. They are told that they have a real choice of faction, yet Tris worries that what the system wants is for them to just "trust the test." After all, the test is supposed to tell them who they are, and this knowledge will help them determine their place in society. Can one really be free to choose their place in society if the test *prescribes* where they fit?

Well, yes and no. It's a limited moral freedom at best, because while they can choose a different faction than the one the test prescribes—or the one they were raised in—their choice of faction at the Choosing Ceremony is the end of their freedom. Becoming an adult and citizen just means acting within the constraints of your faction as the social order demands. But this isn't a robust sense of moral or political freedom. To see this, consider what happens throughout the initial testing process, especially in the case of a Divergent, whose results are inconclusive. Once the test shows them who they're supposed to be, there's no longer hope for the *political freedom* to be themselves, if that doesn't fit current social molds. As Tris's mom states poignantly, "You don't conform, your mind works in a million different ways . . . they are scared of you."

Being who you are will cost a Divergent everything if found out. This leaves a Divergent with two options: death or suppressing who they are. Neither option leads to their wellbeing or being fully alive—in other words, flourishing. The bottom line is this: freedom is essential to flourishing; so if a system radically undermines socio-political freedom through coercion or manipulation, it undermines human flourishing as well.

Another reason to think the faction system is insufficient to promote human flourishing is to consider one faction with its related virtue in isolation from the rest. Candor's virtue is honesty. They speak the truth. Unfortunately, however, truth-telling by itself isn't always good, for we can speak truth in a way that is harmful to the hearer. The movie's narrator highlights this concern when she says that Candor "tell the truth, even when you wish they wouldn't." Of course, we may *need* to hear the truth when we really don't *want* to. Perhaps our physical wellbeing depends on hearing truths about dietary or other life habits that need to be changed. Hearing these words are good for us even if unpleasant. Fair enough, but that isn't the worry here. If those words are spoken with a harsh or mean tone, we can see quickly that honesty needs to be tempered by another virtue such as kindness or compassion, and ultimately be interested in the overall good of the person to whom they speak. In short, emphasizing a single virtue is insufficient to make a faction good for society's flourishing, even if other factions exist to counterbalance its strength.

Roots of Evil

It's tempting to think a social system *alone* can provide the tempering needed for factions to emphasize their virtue in the right way. Perhaps the system can institute strict rules that will keep us from disrupting the prescribed "order." Erudite leader Jeanine Matthews thinks so when she expresses what she believes to be the root of social evil, for which the faction system provides the remedy. Consider the following exchange between her and Tris:

> JEANINE: It's hard to let go [of family] . . . Faction before blood. It's an important ideal, but sometimes difficult to fulfill. It goes against our fundamental human nature; but that's exactly the weakness we need to overcome. . . .
>
> TRIS: You think human nature is weakness.
>
> JEANINE: I think human nature is the enemy. It's human nature to keep secrets, to lie, to steal; and I want to eradicate that. That's how we'll maintain a stable, peaceful society.

For Matthews, there isn't some *aspect* of human nature—for example, character—at the root of our social problems. Human nature *itself* is the real enemy. But even if we pinpoint this as the *root* issue, should we deal with the problem by instituting a system that "eradicates" those who disrupt it? Jeanine's intention to build a stable and peaceful society is admirable, but what she's willing to do to achieve this is ironically part of the problem. Whether creating an out-group of factionless persons who barely scrape by, or ordering the mass extermination of both Divergents and the Abnegation faction, we can see that good intentions worked out through a system won't make for peace, stability, and social flourishing. What we need is a better explanation of the roots of evil so that we can find a better way to overcome corruption and evil.

Throughout the movie we're treated to a vision of human nature that explains the *roots of evil* as being vices or vicious character traits, not human nature itself. Vicious character traits manifest themselves through the choices people make, revealing the kind of person one is. Consider, for example, the related vices of *jealousy and fear* on display in the relationship between Tris and some of the male Dauntless initiates. Tris has worked her way up from the bottom of Dauntless initiates, and others who are struggling to make the cut become jealous of her success. Jealousy leads to fear of failure, and fear of failure leads Al and his buddies to attempt murdering Tris. When the attempted murder fails, and Al realizes that his failure as an initiate is imminent, he takes his own life. The moral of the story is: vices are the roots of evil, and when cultivated, they lead to all kinds of evil acts.

Another example of vice leading to evil acts is the *lust for power and control*. This is portrayed powerfully through both Dauntless leader, Eric, and Erudite leader, Jeanine. Eric wants only to be top dog, the most powerful in his faction. His love of power leads him to treat people as mere means to his ends, and he delights in their weaknesses and failures. His approach is harsh, not affectionate; mean, not kind; cold, not inviting. He's ready and willing to change the rules on a dime to advance his agenda, one that operates on a skewed view of "bravery." For Eric, the brave never grant their opponents mercy by allowing them to surrender. Fighting is always to the death. Bravery of Eric's kind is combined with indifference to the unique value of their opponents and peers.

Likewise, Jeanine loves her position of power, and she's willing to do anything to protect the faction system. She entertains gossip and slander of Abnegation without ever proving their guilt. This leads to her elaborate plan to control the minds of Dauntless so that she can use them to eradicate the Abnegation faction, innocent human persons who are supposedly disrupting the system. Again, the moral of the story is: when vicious character traits are cultivated, evil acts result, and the flourishing— in other words, wellbeing—of society is threatened.

Overcoming Evil with Love and the Beauty of Resistance

How then do we deal with corrupt human nature and promote the freedom and flourishing of all? Social justice activist, John M. Perkins has opined, "Love is the final fight," where *love* is understood as a character disposition to actively seek the good of others, even at a cost to oneself and one's family. Moral Philosophers call it *altruism.*

Unique to this kind of love compared with affection, friendship, or romantic kinds of love is that it's primarily other-oriented and self-sacrificing love. It alone holds the remedy to vicious character traits. For example, if you are unkind to others, learning to sacrificially love others will tend to produce kindness towards others because you'll be concerned about their best interests. Likewise, altruism will help other virtues become focused on the good of others. For example, you will tend to be honest or tell the truth in a way that is helpful and not harmful. Even if this is correct, love of this kind has a way of bringing tension into our human relationships.

We first encounter this in the film when Tris and her family are having dinner before the Choosing Ceremony. Love runs rich and deep within her family. You sense the richness of their deep affection for one another as they eat dinner together. While her parents would like to see them stay in the family's faction, they want Tris and her brother to make a mature choice about what's best for each of them. In other words, there's a kind of love in play that goes beyond *affection* for one's children. *Altruism* is embodied in parents seeking what's best for their children, even if that means they might "lose" them to important social roles that serve the common good.

The apparent loss isn't only from the parents' side of the equation. Tris's brother highlights the children's tension here when he says, "You have to think of the family, but you have to think about yourself." Mature adulthood, where you become free to be yourself for the good of others, often comes with the cost of forsaking—and losing—the comforts of family life. Forsaking doesn't mean disowning them or placing "faction before blood." To forsake is to place your family in a secondary order of importance to the pursuit of common goods, and Tris chooses a faction that will best enable her to be herself and thereby advance these goods.

As the story unfolds, these seeds of love for each other flower into something beautiful, and when society needs Tris and her family to stand against corrupt human nature and a corrupt system, they're ready and able to do so. Whether it's Tris's mother rescuing her only to lose her own life in the escape process, or Tris's father picking up a weapon to storm the headquarters of the evil leaders, her parents are ready and willing to give all they have for the common good. They're model altruists!

Perhaps the relationship between Tris and Four is the most striking example of the power altruism has to free others and restore social order. Their relationship begins as strictly business, though there's a bit of tension between them. Four's first demonstration of *love* for Tris is when he observes her training to improve her fighting skills. She's doing her best, yet her form is poor. Poor form leads to an ill-trained fighter who won't succeed. He cares about her success, so he gives her honest feedback and tips on how to use her size to her advantage, to punch properly and effectively. Honesty, combined with care, motivates her to improve and succeed. Here we find an answer to what Candor needs to help society flourish—honesty arising from the virtue of *love* for the other person's good. If they would only speak the truth with an eye towards what's good for all involved, then everyone would be better for it.

A crucial test of any love relationship occurs when you discover something apparently precarious about the other person. In Four's case, this happens when he learns that Tris is Divergent. Instead of leaving her to be ruined, Four fights for and protects her by helping her train for the upcoming test. Clearly he loves her in a deep sense, one that requires wisdom and risk. He risks being exposed as Divergent, as well as his father being exposed as abusive, yet he willingly reveals his true self by allowing her into his mind to see his fears. As an *altruist,* par excellence, Four is willing to sacrifice all, professionally and personally for her sake.

Four's other-oriented love leads not only to Tris passing the test, but also to their joint effort to overcome Jeanine's evil scheme to wipe out many:

> Amazing isn't it . . . everything that makes up a person . . . all wiped away by chemistry. . . . The brilliance of the faction system is that it removes the threat of anyone exercising their independent will. Divergents threaten that system. Don't get me wrong. There's a certain beauty in your resistance, in your defiance of categorization. It's a beauty we can't afford.

How do Tris and Four defeat the evil wrought by Jeanine on Abnegation and Divergents? Provocatively, their love for innocent human lives and the common good doesn't rule out resistance through the use of force. When human freedom and flourishing are at stake, it seems to require it. Resistance is risky and costly—it almost costs Tris her life at the hands of Four. Perhaps the greatest example of *altruism* and self-sacrificial love in the movie is when Tris breaks through to Four to stop him from killing her. Pointing the gun at herself, she encourages him to pull the trigger. It's okay, because she *loves* him and knows that he would not be taking her life of his own accord but as the result of coercive force. But love breaks through and overcomes. Love breaks through by means of a touch, a penetrating gaze, and a gentle inviting voice expressing care, affection, commitment, and willingness to sacrifice for the other. Love disrupts the oppressive system of mind control and restores Four's freedom so he can help finish dismantling the oppressive system and restore social order.

What then are we willing to sacrifice for a system that offers us reprieve from relational harms? Initially we're tempted to relinquish political freedom for such a system but find that it's susceptible to corruption. Those running the system are vicious and lack the virtues necessary to promote the good of those whom they claim to serve. As such, we see that the system itself needs to be overcome to help us find a better way to solve the problems of life. How is it overcome?

In the end, others-oriented sacrificial *love* has the power to overcome the corrupt system. In short, love alone is the final fight, a costly fight indeed. Family and friends are lost, and in some cases, so is your sense of belonging. Even so, it's a worthy cost, for love alone can overcome evil, restore broken relationships, and make a way to advance the freedom and flourishing of all.

6
Tris's Compassion and the Problem of Evil

TRIP MCCROSSIN

"Decades ago our ancestors realized that it is not political ideology, religious belief, race, or nationalism that is to blame for a warring world," Marcus reminds those assembled for the Choosing Ceremony, our heroine Tris among them, as portrayed early in the first novel in Roth's trilogy. "Rather," he contrasts, "they determined that it was the fault of human personality—of humankind's inclination toward evil, in whatever form that is." They also determined, Marcus continues, that the inclination could be resisted, by systematically resisting the five vices bringing about most, if not all of the evil at the time. And so they devised the "faction" system.

The trilogy as a whole is the story of Tris's struggles in and with this system, as it descends into inter-factional civil war. As it does, it's revealed eventually to be far more problematic in its origin and nature than Marcus lets on, and is replaced finally with something better—or so we're left to hope. As she struggles in these ways, she struggles also with the possibility that there are limitations she must accept in the process, to human nature generally, and human reason in particular.

"Human beings as a whole cannot be good for long," she learns from her mom, "before the bad creeps back in and poisons us again." "Human reason can excuse any evil," she learns from her dad, which is "why it's so important that we don't rely on it." As Tris struggles with *the problem of the evil that is civil war*, she struggles also with the *problem of evil* itself, in its modern incarnation. And as we identify with her as our heroine, we're reminded that *we* struggle with it too, and may, through her, come to a better understanding of it.

There's much in Tris's complex storyline, in the original novels, and as they have since been interpreted in film, to contribute to such an understanding. Let's look at two related scenes in the first novel. The first is Tris's approach to her greatest fear in the final fear landscape, which she must negotiate in order to complete her Dauntless initiation. The second sees her re-adopting the same approach again in her struggle later on with simulation-bound Tobias, in struggling more generally to end the war, or at least the slaughter that's begun it.

What links these scenes, and links them in turn to Tris's final struggle at the end of the third novel, is a lesson that she learns from Tobias about the relationship between selflessness and courage, echoing nicely a lesson she learns from her dad about the power of self-sacrifice. The link has sadly been lost as the scenes have been transferred to film. The second of the above scenes is now dissociated from the first. It's associated instead, and not uninterestingly, with Tobias's approach to the portion of his own fear landscape that has to do with the killing of innocents. And the loss is only made worse by the movie's reinterpretation of the death of Tris's mom, from overt self-sacrifice to more routine casualty of war. Still, in the scenes in question, as Roth has laid them out in the original book, she has left a moral complexity hidden for us to discover, one that clarifies Tris's character, as not only defined by, but also *a response to* the problem of evil.

A Tale of Two Traditions

Commonly phrased as the question, "why do bad things happen to good people, and good things to bad?," the problem of evil began its life as a theological one, as far back as the Old Testament's Book of Job—how may we reconcile faith in God's wisdom, power, and benevolence with the misery we regularly suffer nonetheless?

The problem of evil is also a modern *secular* one—as Susan Neiman has convincingly argued in her 2002 book, *Evil in Modern Thought*—which poses a threat not to God's standing, but to human reason. How, that is, can we make reasonable sense of the world, if we can't make sense of it teeming with unreasonable suffering? Whatever other problems Tris may have, she clearly has this one.

To fit Tris into the long conversation about the problem of evil in this way is to ask, in effect, where she falls in the history of competing modern *responses* to the problem. This history is dominated mostly by two sorts of perspectives, Rousseau's and Voltaire's, beginning with their public dispute midway through the eighteenth century.

Rousseau insisted perhaps most fundamentally that we aren't naturally corrupt, but rather are so by virtue of what we make of ourselves in society. "*All* is good leaving the hands of the author of things," he famously tells us at the outset of *Émile*, "but degenerates in human hands." For Rousseau, the genius of this perspective is that our redemption is in our own hands, if only we choose to *reason* our way into a new sense of ourselves, out of a new sense of the long and winding course of humanity's corruption. This is not to say that he thought that such redemption wasn't a complicated and uncertain business. Nor would he deny that it's become only more difficult for us, given the long run of stunning atrocities we've accumulated. If we include the Purity Wars, Tris and company are even worse off.

Perhaps we do better, Tris might think, to follow instead the lead that Voltaire provides in *Candide*. Its namesake, Candide, famously suffers page after page of trial and tribulation. He's accompanied along the way by Dr. Pangloss, droning on endlessly about how in spite of it all, reason compels us to the view that our world is nonetheless the best of all possible worlds. We just have to buck up, as it were, and see our various misfortunes in this light, and thus not nearly so bad after all. To the typical reader's astonishment, Candide takes the bait over and over again, until in the end he just can't do it any longer. Finally, the evidence from our experience compels him to the view that it's *not* reason, but rather *work* that distances us from the "three great evils, boredom, vice, and need."

Rousseau's and Voltaire's opposing responses to the problem of evil animate our intellectual history, which history now includes *Divergent*. The tradition of responses inspired by Rousseau insists, as Neiman puts it, that "morality demands that we make evil intelligible." The one inspired by Voltaire insists instead that "morality demands that we don't." And so the question, again, is whether Tris is cast more from Rousseau's mold or from Voltaire's.

In these terms, in her near-constant insistence that the evil she and others face be made intelligible, Tris is clearly cut from Rousseau's mold. The evil that she believes Tobias's parents represent, for example, isn't properly intelligible in the way that he understands them. And she won't rest until she's convinced him of this, even if it means risking his love and respect; perhaps also her freedom and even her life. Being cut from Rousseau's mold in this sense is also at the heart of Tris's struggle in, and eventually with the faction system.

All Is Good Leaving the Hands of the Ancestors. Or Maybe Not

Humanity's "inclination toward evil, in whatever form that is," according to the ancestors Marcus harkens back to during his address at the Choosing Ceremony, is what's "to blame for a warring world." These same ancestors, he continues, had a specific understanding of "evil, in whatever form." Identifying five such forms primarily—selfishness, aggression, duplicity, cowardice, and ignorance—they divided society into five distinct "factions," each devoted to "eradicating" one of these five vices, by championing one of the opposing virtues. And so, the Abnegation pursue selflessness, the Amity peacefulness, the Candor honesty, the Dauntless bravery, and the Erudite intelligence. In pursuing their designated virtue, each faction suits itself nicely to fulfilling a particular role, or set of related roles in moving "toward a better society and a better world." In one or another faction, Marcus concludes, citizens help to repair "the world's disarray," and in the process "find meaning . . . find purpose . . . find life." "Apart from them," he adds, as if both to comfort and to warn, society "would not survive."

But survival isn't guaranteed *with* them either—sadly, for society generally, and for Tris in particular. At first, as the system descends into inter-factional civil war, she struggles against the war's principal instigator, Jeanine Matthews—not only because innocents have been targeted, but because she herself has become a *high-value* target. Because Tris is Divergent she doesn't fit neatly into a single one of the system's five factions, and so is less easily controlled. But working to defeat the evil that is Jeanine isn't a simple matter. In order to succeed, Tris must struggle against Jeanine and two other evils: Tobias's estranged parents, Marcus Eaton and Evelyn Johnson.

Marcus, who leads the Abnegation, abused Tobias as a child. Evelyn, who leads the factionless, abandoned him. Tris's and Tobias's feelings about them couldn't be clearer at this point in the storyline. In order to defeat mass murderer and enslaver Jeanine, though, Tris must side with one or the other, Marcus the abuser or Evelyn the abandoner; the choice made only more difficult by Tobias having sided with Evelyn. What Tris must do, and in fact does, in a manner that would surely make Rousseau proud, is to "make intelligible" the evils in question.

This she does by determining, with uncanny certainty, that the evils represented by Jeanine, Marcus, and Evelyn must all be a function of something broader historically. What this turns out to be is what Marcus has convinced her is "information that will change everything." In the end she succeeds only by convincing Tobias of this as well: that the only way to struggle against evil, in any or all of the ways presented by Jeanine, Marcus, and Evelyn, is to learn something deeper about it, and in the process about ourselves. Only then can they sort out what best to do about it.

Definitely Not. Information Changes Everything

Among the remarkable things about the trilogy as a whole is the surprise we experience along with Tris and company, as we hear Amanda Ritter, soon to be Edith Prior explain more fully the origin and intent of the faction system. It's a story, fleshed out in *Allegiant*, of genetic technology gone awry, tragically compromising the moral fabric of a large portion of the US population, limiting them to embodying primarily only one of the five virtues. It's a story that leads ultimately to the "Purity Wars," between the genetically "pure" and genetically "damaged." It's a story that also makes new sense, to Tris and to us, of her Divergence.

According to Amanda's deeper story, Divergence is far from being the danger that Jeanine labels it. Rather, being simply an aptitude for multiple virtues, it's really no more than a marker for genetic integrity. With this evolutionary clue in mind, the ancestors decided to isolate the populations of certain cities and chemically "reset" their memories, to replace them with a scenario of living peacefully in isolation. The reset came with instructions, to be passed down from one generation of city leaders to the next; that once Divergence became sufficiently prevalent the "experiment" would end. At this point, its population would rejoin the general population, allowing natural selection to do its business. Marcus held up the faction system as almost divine inspiration, but it turns out to have merely instrumental value, as a way to help the process by rendering city life more peaceful than it might otherwise have been.

Once the truth about divergence and the factions is revealed, Tris's struggle eventually becomes saving not the system, but its citizens from a sort of death from mass "resetting" of their memories. In the process, shockingly, she dies. Shocking, because it has to seem to us that Roth could easily enough have imagined a similar, but less upsetting ending. Caleb could have died instead, for example, as we're led to anticipate. The trilogy might have ended less unhappily, then, with Tris and Tobias having a version of the conversation that instead he has with himself. But it didn't. And *that* it didn't, *that* she died, draws us naturally to *how* she died, completing the storyline begun in *Divergent* with Tobias's lesson about the relationship between selflessness and courage, echoing as it does her dad's lesson about the power of self-sacrifice. It helped her to become Dauntless, and later to defeat Jeanine. And now, again, it helps her to defeat the Bureau. It all comes down to the power of Tris's compassion—and, we have to believe, our own.

Is Tris Channeling Émile?

The faction system, as Marcus presents it and as Amanda later re-presents it, can be understood as reflecting a particular strain in Rousseau's writing. The first line of *Émile* above, "*All is good leaving the hands of the author of things, but degenerates in human hands,*" is meant to summarize his perspective in an earlier work, *On the Origin and Foundations of Inequality*. Here, he addressed in detail the origin and development of, to use again Marcus's language, "humankind's inclination to evil, in whatever form." For Rousseau, what's "to blame for a warring world," most fundamentally, is a growing imbalance over the course of human history. This imbalance is between what he takes to be two basic human instincts: to preserve and promote *ourselves*, and to act compassionately toward *others*. In making evil intelligible, reason can't help but find the former steadily overwhelming the latter, from our earliest time. And the result of such an imbalance is eventually "wars, battles, murders, and reprisals, which shock nature and outrage reason," such as the Purity Wars.

Rousseau's approach to fixing this, generally speaking, is to redress the imbalance, or at least compensate for it. He develops this into two distinct strategies, which he lays out in *Of the Social Contract* and *Émile*. In the first, in the spirit of what brings about the faction system, we are to "take people as they are, and make laws as they can be," in order to rein in our inclination to evil—even while leaving the inclination otherwise intact. In the second, to paraphrase, we take laws as they are, and make *people* as they can be, as they *ought to be*, through a radical manner of educating them from infancy, in isolation from the corrupting influences of society. While distinct, the strategies are clearly *related*—two sides, as it were, of the same coin—which brings us back around to Tris.

If Rousseau were a *Divergent* fan, he might remind us at this point of the warning Tris's mom gives her, adding emphasis to it, that humanity "*as a whole* cannot be good for long, before the bad creeps back in and poisons *us* again." So the challenge of establishing a social contract, in order to *make* us good, is not just to make us good in the short term, but make our goodness stick! Whatever peace is made possible by the social contract, though, she's telling us, is susceptible still to such creeping poison. And the only way we can stop its creeping in is to reclaim compassion as a countervailing virtue, keeping in check our otherwise overwhelming instinct to preserve and promote ourselves at the expense of others. But if the odds are against us, as it seems, how do we muster the courage to make the attempt?

If only we could witness even just one person growing up to embody a proper balance of compassion and self-preservation and self-promotion, then we could imagine others following suit. Then we could imagine wiser folks available to perform the fundamental roles within the social contract—keeping the creeping poison at bay and the social contract thriving. But we have *already* in Émile, Rousseau would insist, just such a person. So, is Tris to *Divergent* what Émile is to *Émile*?

The Meanings of Selflessness

"What did Tobias tell me?" Tris asks herself, facing her worst fear in her final Dauntless initiation test. Her greatest fear is that innocents will die as a result of her choices, worst of all her family. And so her challenge is to choose properly, by Dauntless standards, between slaughtering her family and being killed herself, by Jeanine, who holds a gun to her temple. "*Selflessness and bravery aren't that different*," she recalls Tobias telling her, and in this she finds her strategy. To prove her bravery, she chooses to sacrifice her own life for the sake of her family's life. "*Shoot me instead*," she insists, lowering her gun and turning to press her forehead to the barrel of Jeanine's gun. A "click, and a bang," she awakes, and she's passed.

But does the "click, and a bang" mean that *she* was shot, or was mom, dad, or Caleb; or was the gun shooting blanks, or fired into the air? Tris doesn't know, and we don't either. However well we choose, the world and others in it may not cooperate quite as we'd like.

When later she again takes up the same strategy, in her confrontation with simulation-controlled Tobias, she's more aware that it may not pan out as before. And this has to be all the more true when she puts herself in the way of a gun yet again, David's this time as the storyline concludes, in order to keep Caleb out of harm's way—this time to tragically fatal effect.

It all starts with her memory of Tobias's "theory that selflessness and bravery aren't all that different." "All your life you've been training to forget yourself," he explains, highlighting Tris's Abnegation upbringing, "so when you're in danger, it becomes your first instinct." But it's *not* her first *and only* instinct. Courage allows us to move forward to do this or that *come what may*, but it's not what moves us in the first place, if we have the courage to do this or that *particular* thing.

Sometimes, we *put ourselves* in harm's way—by jumping onto moving trains, scaling tall buildings, sliding crazily down a wire strung from the top of the tallest, and so on. In such moments, we're not being self*less*, but self*ish*, though in a benign sense of doing for ourselves, simply for our own sake. But these benignly selfish acts aren't at anyone else's expense. Still, such benign self*ish*ness is indeed, as Tobias suggests, made easier by self*less*ness; in that to be selfless is to abandon, at least partially, the care we naturally have to preserve and promote ourselves.

Sometimes, we're *put* in harm's way, or the harm we put ourselves in the way of is worse than anticipated. In these moments, our instinct is to escape, preferably unharmed. To be courageous is to be undaunted by the possibility that the harm may in fact be realized. Again, selflessness helps us to set aside our natural inclination to preserve and promote ourselves, and so to make an earnest attempt at escape more likely than simply curling up and whimpering.

And sometimes, finally, we *witness others* in harm's way, and our instinct is to relieve the resulting distress, even if this puts us in harm's way in turn. Here again, courage *allows* us to act, and again selflessness facilitates this, by helping us to set aside self-preservation and self-promotion, allowing us to turn more readily toward, rather than away from the danger. And the motivator here is none other than the virtue that Rousseau thinks is so pivotal—that is, *compassion*.

Selflessness facilitates courage, but courage is most meaningfully deployed where the motivation isn't self-interested, but compassionately in the interest of others. And in this, we're reminded of the portion of the Dauntless Manifesto that Will introduces Tris to, and which becomes for her a source of enduring fascination: "We believe in ordinary acts of bravery, in the courage that drives one person to stand up for another." Except, the point here being, it's *not* bravery that *drives* us to do so, but rather *allows* us to, if we're already driven by our compassion toward them to perform such "ordinary acts" on their behalf.

Tris's storyline traces her path from Initiate to Insurgent to Allegiant, developing as she goes the heroic qualities that will allow her finally to transcend such categories and act to save her people. She does so in an extraordinary, and as her dad would say powerful, gesture of self-sacrifice. Integral to her moral progress, and to the people's salvation, and the opportunity to rebuild "a better society and a better world," is her embrace of selflessness as a vehicle for courage *and* her compassion as its motivation.

Without the two scenes we've focused on, in the first of which Tris acts to keep safe her family and then Tobias, and the second of which she struggles with David to keep safe from harm the city in general, and Caleb in particular, the storyline doesn't have the same powerful effect. What wouldn't have been realized, that is, at least in the way it was, is the possibility of a better life for all without the factions and without genetically-driven prejudice. And integral to these scenes, as we've unpacked them, is the idea that Tris's acts are *compassionate* acts. In Tris's world, as in Émile's, acting out of sincere and careful reasoning *and* compassion is what will save us from ourselves.

What Tris's storyline adds to Émile's, and adds provocatively, is the dimension of courage. Imagining again Rousseau as a *Divergent* fan, might he not think to himself that perhaps he should have added a wartime storyline to *Émile*? Doing so might have given Émile a chance to play more overtly the part of the hero, and so to be a more obvious role model in reconstructing society—as Tris seems to us, more and more as the overall storyline proceeds, and then in the end to Tobias as well, and through him to the rest of us even more so.

"There are so many ways to be brave in this world," Tobias tells us, in the raw immediacy of Tris's death. These naturally include *her* ways, most notably "laying down your life for something bigger than yourself, or for someone else." But they also include the more routine bravery she inspires in him, which is "gritting your teeth through pain, and the work of every day, the slow walk toward a better life." As we hear in his last lines, though, a few years into his "slow walk," he seems also inspired now by the *manner* of her bravery. He's also inspired by the routine kindness and compassion of Christina and others close to him, in their newly liberated city, which Tris's compassion and bravery made possible. "Life damages us, every one," he learned from a young age, but now he's learning something new, inspired by Tris's selflessness making possible both her compassion and the bravery to act on it. "We can be mended," he insists. But he means this not in the passive sense of the Bureau's project. Rather, we can and should pay better attention to one another, to our various distresses, and to relieving them, courageously if need be. "We mend each other."

The lesson for us? We'd best be like Tris, and Tobias now also, smart, selfless, brave, *and* compassionate, if *we're* to "mend each other," if the "long walk to a better life" is to be *our* walk.[1]

---

[1] I'd like to dedicate this chapter to my colleague Mark Colby, who passed away tragically prematurely while I was working to complete it. He will be greatly missed.

7
Give Peace a Chance

COURTLAND LEWIS

The Dauntless Manifesto exclaims:

WE BELIEVE
that peace is hard-won, that sometimes it is necessary to fight for peace. But more than that:

WE BELIEVE
that justice is more important than peace.

It's true that peace is often hard-won, and there are times when we must fight for it. The great advocate for peace, Mahatma Gandhi, maintains throughout *The Essential Writings of Mahatma Gandhi* that there's value in armed resistance, as long as it's done in defense of a good cause. Another pillar of the Peace Movement, Martin Luther King, Jr., details beautifully in his "Letter from a Birmingham Jail" that we must all *struggle* against ignorance and injustice—"Injustice anywhere is a threat to justice everywhere." So, with Gandhi and King on our side, it's safe to conclude that the first part of the Dauntless Manifesto is true.

The problem with the Dauntless Manifesto, and by extension the thinking of those who created Chicago's faction system, is the claim that justice is something so different from peace that it's *more important*. If you think about it, it's hard to even make sense of the claim that justice and peace are different. For instance, when justice is carried out, that's what we typically call "keeping the peace." Maybe the mistake is the result of instances when justice is carried out, yet we don't like

67

the outcome, cry "foul," and begin demanding "real justice." This explanation doesn't work because all we mean by 'real justice' is "I want so-and-so punished in such a way that makes me feel good," and that isn't justice. It's more like a sick perversion, a desire to see and delight in others' suffering. Justice is something entirely different.

So, with this glaring problem, is the Dauntless Manifesto still valuable? "Yes." Even though it mistakenly assumes justice and peace are different, it illuminates several complex conceptual issues of justice and peace. In fact, if we look closely enough we'll see it grounds a rich and pro-active conception of justice, what Nicholas Wolterstorff calls shalom.

Pass the Peace Serum, Man . . .

'Peace' is used throughout Veronica Roth's *Divergent* series. The faction system, which orders Chicago, is in fact designed to create peace. After a devastating war that led Chicagoans to segregate themselves from the rest of the world, it was thought that breaking up into specialized factions would ensure the peace of society. Since all factions working together should achieve peace, each faction has some sort of individual commitment to peace.

The Amity Manifesto states that for the sake of keeping the peace, you shouldn't think negative thoughts about people, even if the thoughts you have happen to be true. Not only would this conception of peace fail to cut it in Candor, but it doesn't create peace. On the outside Amity are peaceful, but on the inside they must be bursting with inner-turmoil. Luckily, they have *peace* serum to help them through this turmoil or they would be a much different faction. So, their concept of peace is sort of like the stereotypical Sixties hippie counter-culture, whose devotees lived off the land, played a lot of music, and practiced peace and love—with the help of their own cannabis-based peace serum.

The Erudite rely on knowledge to avoid conflict. The peace they hope to obtain is the peace of negotiation and logical agreement. Their belief is that if we take emotions and sentimentality out of the social equation and seek logical solutions to our problems, especially when we feel we've been wronged, we'll arrive at a peaceful solution. Candor is similar, in the sense that if we rely on truth instead of lies, deception, and emotion, we're more likely to avoid war and find peace.

Abnegation takes a completely different approach, crafting a type of asceticism—a denial of the self—in order to focus on the needs of others. For them, if we get rid of the self, and we meet the needs of others, there'll be no motive for violence and war. So, once the self is gone, the only thing left is peace. Similarly, Dauntless courage focuses on the needs of others, for their overriding purpose is to defend the weak and powerless in society.

With the prominence of "peace" throughout Chicago, you'd think there would be a highly developed conception of peace studied, understood, and promoted by each faction, but there isn't one. Though each conception of peace shares similarities with the others, they're not the same. Amity's "peace" is simply a drug-induced lack of conflict. Granted, they're the most secure faction because they control the source of food, but overall, their life is pretty meaningless. The fact that they must drug themselves in order to maintain peace, not only implies the fragility of their faction, but it suggests their peace is merely an illusion.

The peace that comes as a result of a knowledgeable and truthful dialogue, like the sort in which Erudite and Candor engage, is completely different from the euphoric peace of Amity. Abnegation's "peace" shares similarities with Amity, since the denial of self and the loss of the self—via peace serum—resemble the same phenomenon, but Abnegation's peace involves a conscious self-denial, while Amity's peace involves a euphoric ignorance of the self. Since each faction appears to be working with a different conception of peace, it's no wonder their society is a tinderbox waiting to ignite—they're striving for different things!

What about Dauntless peace? Their conception of peace is unclear. From certain things seen in the Manifesto, and mentioned by Tris and Four, peace for the Dauntless occurs when people get what they need or deserve. If this is true, then peace mirrors justice, since justice simply means "you get what you deserve." But the Dauntless Manifesto says peace and justice are two different things! So, we're at an impasse. Instead of running away from it like a stoned Amity, let's be brave Dauntless and face it like our deepest fear.

J-U-S-T-I-C-E, What Does Justice Mean for Me?

Let's take a break from talking about peace, and talk about justice. Wolterstorff notes in his own trilogy of books on justice—*Until Justice and Peace Embrace, Justice: Rights and Wrongs*, and *Justice in Love*, the third-century Roman jurist Ulpian defined justice—*iustitia*—as "a steady and enduring will to render to each his or her *ius*—right." Stated differently, justice requires that each person get what they deserve.

Long before Ulpian, Aristotle had discussed justice in *The Politics*. Within this work, he distinguishes between three types of particular justice: distributive, compensatory, and retributive. Distributive justice focuses on how best to distribute the benefits and burdens of society. In other words, when organizing a society, distributive justice attempts to ensure everyone is treated equally. This doesn't mean that everyone has the same amount of money or status, nor does it imply "redistribution;" but rather, it strives to ensure everyone has access to the basic goods they require to satisfy their needs and to flourish.

A prime example of this is Roth's Chicago, at least the way we understand it at the beginning of *Divergent*. According to the original tale, the city founders distributed the benefits and burdens of society along faction lines, five main factions and one group known as the factionless. Theoretically, everyone has a social task to perform, based on the innate virtue they exhibit, and if everyone carries out their individual social duty, society as a whole will be just. Of course, we should question whether or not the factionless carry an undue social burden, but at least on the surface, their basic needs are met. As the series develops evidence suggests otherwise, but I'll hold off on discussing the factionless until later.

The other two types of justice address what should happen after wrongdoing. Compensatory justice deals with what victims are owed, while retributive justice deals with what wrongdoers are owed—in other words, it deals with proper punishment.

Retributive justice is the most common form of justice discussed in contemporary America. Retributive justice attempts to explain what should happen in the wake of some wrongdoing. Retributive justice is most often associated with legality, since if you break a law and get caught, the law prescribes what you deserve. When the punishment accurately fits the crime, we call that justice. Our laws don't always match the wrongdoing, and so when the punishment doesn't fit the crime, we feel as though an injustice has occurred. Furthermore, if a person commits a crime and they don't receive any punishment, then an injustice has no doubt occurred. Though legal discussions are interesting, we're concerned with morality not legality. Things become much more difficult when we examine moral justice.

In terms of morality, we don't have a clear set of rules of retribution. To be honest, the legal rules of punishment aren't that clear, but thanks to centuries of legal precedent, we have a semi-objective framework in which to punish wrongdoers. Unrefined moral beliefs, on the other hand, are often much more subjective, and depend upon familial tradition, popular culture, and just about anything else. If someone tries to kill you, like Al tries to kill Tris, what's the appropriate moral response? Should you try to kill him, ignore him, punch him, slowly poison him, kill one of his relatives, get the authorities to punish him, or should you forgive him? To be capable of answering these sorts of questions we need a moral framework that explains the nature of wrongdoing. Moral theories of justice attempt to offer such an explanation.

The Moral Landscape of Justice

As Robert Solomon eloquently illustrates in *A Passion for Justice*, justice isn't just some abstract concept; it's something we practice with every decision we make. Understanding justice in this way requires that we see justice as a *relational* concept, which makes perfect sense when you think about it. If Jeanine were the only person in existence, then she would be incapable of harming anyone else. So, it wouldn't make sense to say she deserves something from someone else, or that she owes another person something—there's no one to owe or be owed. For justice to be applicable to a case, there must be a relationship between moral agents.

In terms of wrongdoing, there must be an agent, like Jeanine, and a recipient of Jeanine's wrongdoing, like Tris. To illustrate the point, Wolterstorff uses the *principle of correla-*

tives as a representational formulation of this sort of moral relationship:

> If Tris is the sort of entity that has rights, like a human, then Jeanine has an obligation to help or refrain from wronging Tris, if and only if Jeanine has a right against Tris for her to help or refraining from wronging Jeanine in the same way.

What the principle shows is that both Jeanine and Tris share the same moral status, and because they're morally equal, they should both respect the rights of each other. To respect the rights of each other requires that they do, or refrain from doing, certain actions. When they respect each other's rights, a state of justice exists between them.

Based on Roth's narrative, Jeanine fails to respect not only Tris's rights but also the population of Chicago's rights. As a result, what starts off as a society that on the surface seems just, devolves into a near-complete state of injustice. To avoid injustice, moral agents must both take into consideration their own personal rights *and* the personal rights of the recipients of their action, or inaction. Jeanine pays lip-service to the idea that her mass atrocity is for the good of others, that it's what Chicago deserves, but she really only considers her own needs—the desire to rid Chicago of what *she* considers "undesirables." We even see that she uses Dauntless as a mere tool to kill and prop up her immoral dictatorship. She neither cares about their principles nor their integrity. She just wants the power to shape the world according to her own desires.

Of course, Dauntless principles make their co-operation with Jeanine perplexing. The one faction that is designed to fight for peace and justice becomes the faction fighting for oppression and injustice. The only way this glaring inconsistency makes sense is to show that Jeanine's "justice" is more important than the peace of letting Abnegation, Divergents, and the factionless exist. In other words, if justice is more important than peace, then Jeanine has the conceptual groundwork to justify her mass atrocity. For justice to be more important than peace, peace must allow for injustice. So, those who commit injustice deserve punishment, and retributive justice allows us to disturb the peace of those who participate in *injustice*. That's a mind-full, even for an Erudite! Let's see how it plays out.

Here's what a defender of Jeanine might say: Jeanine wants peace, and the only way for her to achieve it is to punish—retributive justice—the Abnegation and Divergents who threaten Chicago's peace. Even though her actions appear to be doing great harm to Chicago and its citizens, they actually achieve justice by sacrificing the peace of wrongdoers, in order to ensure the peace of society. This is Jeanine's best defense, but it all rests on whether or not Abnegation and Divergents are guilty of Jeanine's accusations of wrongdoing, and that the peace she envisions will be peaceful and just.

Abnegation and Divergents aren't guilty of the crimes of which they're accused. In fact, we find out later on that Divergents are society's hope for future peace. So, the first part of her defense fails. Still, maybe her "peace" is worth the atrocity? Since she uses an armed fighting force, drugged and manipulated by propaganda and mind-control, it's safe to say that her vision of peace lacks wide support. In fact, the use of propaganda and manipulation implies her vision of Chicago probably lacks any support, outside of those who hope to ride her coattails to supremacy. If this is true, then the Chicago Jeanine envisions will be one of manipulation, armed oppression, and fear. The greatest mark against Jeanine is that the Chicago at the beginning of *Divergent* is obviously more peaceful than the one at the end of the book. Furthermore, peace requires a certain amount of freedom, especially from being oppressed and executed. Justice requires the same, since one doesn't deserve execution for speaking truth to power. So, the second part of her defense fails. We're, then, faced with the conclusion that Jeanine's vision for a "peaceful" Chicago isn't peaceful.

Give Shalom a Chance

Just like the Divergent Series, I've said a lot about peace, but I haven't actually discussed what it is and how it would manifest in a complex society like Chicago. Peace must be something more than Amity's conception. If Amity is correct, then we'd be forced to say that drug addicts or people with dementia accurately represent peace. Sure, we sometimes speak of them as "being at peace" or "looking peaceful," but that's not the type of peace associated with justice. The peace related to justice, and the one that Chicago hopes to achieve, is a peace of action—one that requires caring for the needs of others and ourselves.

Distributive justice assumes there's a possible state of affairs where people have their needs met, and justice calls each of us to strive towards creating this state of affairs. Wolterstorff discusses such a state, specifically in terms of the Abrahamic religious traditions of Judaism, Christianity, and Islam. For the God of Abraham, justice occurs when moral beings receive that to which they have a right—it's the same idea seen in Ulpian's definition of justice. Wolterstorff shows that the Hebrew term 'shalom', translated as *peace*, was used by the Israelites as the representation of God's justice on Earth. Most Jews, Christians, and Muslims, in some way or another, have accepted the same idea. Of course, over the centuries the concept has morphed, changed, and in some cases been abandoned by the followers of the Abrahamic tradition; but the concept of shalom, as accurately describing a form of peace based on distributive justice remains. It's valuable because it provides a conceptual understanding of an ethical community working together to achieve a just state of affairs that creates peace. The good news is you don't have to be religious to accept shalom. In fact, as Ulpian demonstrates, all you need in order to accept this conception of peace is to entertain the belief that there are moral agents who have needs, and when these needs are met, peace occurs.

If we apply shalom to the *Divergent* series, we see that when Tris receives what she deserves—food, water, respect, not being killed, a state of shalom occurs. In other words, when justice occurs, peace occurs. To use Wolterstorff's terminology, "peace and justice embrace" when the needs of moral agents are met. But this is only half of the story, for shalom isn't merely about Tris's peace. Rather, Tris must also be engaged in ensuring others achieve shalom too. In fact, according to this understanding of peace, all moral agents are required to foster the peace of themselves and others. Wolterstorff describes it in the following way: "In shalom, each person enjoys justice, enjoys his or her rights. There is no shalom without justice. . . . Shalom is the human being dwelling at peace in all his or her relationships: with God, with self, with fellows, with nature." Granted, we might never achieve a perfect state of peace, where all of our needs and the needs of others are met, but we can achieve it to certain degrees and in certain instances.

This should all sound familiar, since this is exactly the type of justice for which Tris is fighting and that is seen in the Dauntless Manifesto. It also seems to be the basis of Roth's Chicago; for if each faction combines their virtues in the right way, without excluding the factionless, then we'll have a situation where shalom can occur.

Distributive Dauntless Justice

What would a peaceful Chicago look like? Well, it would look like the Chicago envisioned in the Dauntless Manifesto, minus the claim that implies peace and justice are somehow different. So, let's change the Manifesto to say: **We Believe** that justice and peace occur at the same time, that you can't have one without the other. With this subtle, yet important change, it becomes clear that the Dauntless faction is concerned with distributive justice. They're fighting for a state in which all citizens have their rights respected and exist in a state of peace.

Here are some excerpts from the Dauntless Manifesto, found in Roth's *World of Divergent: The Path to Allegiant*, which illustrate what they hope to achieve for Chicago:

WE BELIEVE
it is necessary to fight for peace, in freedom from fear,
in the courage that drives one person to stand up for another;
in defending those who cannot defend themselves;
in bold deeds.

WE DO NOT BELIEVE
in empty heads, empty mouths, or empty hands;
that we should be allowed to stand idly by.

The major theme throughout the Dauntless Manifesto is to be brave in the face of injustice, and each statement deals with fighting injustice in some way or avoiding the traps that allow injustice to occur. So, they aren't concerned with the justice associated with punishment. In fact, the claim that "justice is more important than peace" is the only claim that comes close to being about punishment, and as seen above with the discussion of

Jeanine's "peace," it takes some pretty big conceptual leaps to ground such a claim.

Instead of punishment, the Dauntless are dedicated to fighting to see that all persons have their individual needs met within the complex social system of Chicago. Their Manifesto is a call to justice: to fight for peace, to stand up for the rights of others, to defend those rights in the face of personal loss, to think and work hard to see no one goes hungry, and to never stand idly by while injustice occurs. Therefore, their Manifesto is a call to shalom—justice that creates peace.

The Dauntless envision and are designed to fight for an *ethical community* where individuals are afforded the opportunity to enjoy that to which they have a right. And even though the Dauntless have taken it on their shoulders—as their central virtue—to fight for peace, they can't do it alone. *Everyone* in Chicago must also fight for peace. As King was quoted saying at the beginning of this chapter, "Injustice anywhere is a threat to justice everywhere." So, peace and justice must be part of each faction, both fighting for and destroying barriers to both. Peace can't be secured in an unjust situation by managing to get everyone in society to feel content with their lot in life. As Wolterstorff maintains, peace would not have been present *even if* all the blacks in the United States had been content in their state of slavery; it would not be present in South Africa *even if* all the blacks felt happy. This seems to be the closest Jeanine's Chicago could ever get to peace, which is no peace at all. The Dauntless have a much nobler and sustainable conception of peace in mind.

Chicago's Ethical Community

The brilliance of Roth's Chicago is that it's designed to create shalom, a place of peace and justice. The factions have all of the pieces present to achieve it. Just as we saw with the Dauntless Manifesto, if we make a few changes we get a more just Dauntless, based on a clearer understanding justice. If we make a few changes to Chicago's faction system, we get a more just society with a clearer vision of peace.

The first thing that needs to be done is to welcome the factionless into society as equals. If they want to perform the service oriented jobs of Chicago, that's fine. Tending to the basic needs of society, as maintenance workers and garbage collectors, is just as important as farming and performing research. When I was young, I was always told to work hard so I wouldn't become a "ditch digger." As an adult, I've known several "ditch diggers" and they live rewarding, flourishing lives. So, we shouldn't look down upon the jobs of the factionless through biased eyes. To help this, Chicago should create a sixth faction based on service to the city—maybe call it Amenity or Beneficence.

On the other hand, if the factionless want to apply their skills to something else, they should be allowed the social mobility to develop their particular virtues. One way to address their lack of social mobility is to allow people who fail at one faction's initiation test to join a different faction. This would cut down on the number of factionless, and if the factionless become their own faction, then we would no longer have an "outcast" portion of society. I could go on, but I'll let Tobias and the other post-*Allegiant* leaders figure out the details of their new social system.

Assuming we can successfully incorporate the factionless into society as equals, we're left with the faction system itself. With a more complete conception of justice and peace in place, the following changes should be made in order to allow for each faction to enhance each other's and their own virtues.

The strength of Amity is their ability to foster peace, but as seen earlier, getting stoned isn't peace. They need to work more closely with the Dauntless to identify basic needs and provide food for all of the citizens of Chicago. They should also work with Candor and Erudite to teach them a more peaceful way of being honest and intelligent. Being honest doesn't mean that you have to be unkind. Amity could teach Candor how to be compassionate with their honesty, and they could teach Erudite the same lesson in regards to intelligence. It's easy to forget the human factor when all you do is look at data. Amity could help remind the Erudite of real human needs, which would not only help them become more intelligent, but more wise.

At the same time, Amity could learn a more meaningful way of life that doesn't require peace serum. Candor could teach them how to be more open and honest about their feelings, and Erudite could teach them methods of dealing with disagreement.

Abnegation . . . let's face it, they're about as close to perfection as you can get. Roth paints them that way, and I tend to agree. The biggest lesson they need to learn is that you can't love others if you don't love yourself. Dauntless could teach them how to be a little more self-centered—that it's okay to not be so . . . *stiff*. At the same time, Abnegation could teach Dauntless not to be so self-centered, that sometimes it's alright to be modest and have good manners.

What am I trying to say? It all comes down to the simple fact that we all need to be a little more Divergent and a lot more dedicated to peace and justice. There's nothing wrong with promoting one virtue above the rest. We all have talents and skills, and we should promote their development. Nevertheless, variety is good too. We should learn and practice the virtues we lack—even if we plan on never using them—because they give us a better understanding of our own strengths and weaknesses. By branching out we learn about the needs and wants of others, and we learn about our own. As a result, we become wiser and more capable of promoting and achieving shalom.

These are just some suggestions, but they seem to be the missing pieces that allow Roth's Chicago to devolve into war, and they might be their only means to find peace and justice in the future. I dare say, the same might be true for us too![1]

---

[1] I would like to professionally thank Nicholas Wolterstorff for his wonderful contributions to philosophy and theology, and personally thank him for his support and contribution to my peace while working on my doctorate.

III

Today We Choose

8
Plato's Chicago

GREG LITTMANN

This day marks a happy occasion—the day on which we receive our new initiates, who will work with us toward a better society and a better world.

—MARCUS EATON (*Divergent*)

How should society be arranged? As citizens in democracies, it's a question we can't avoid. We have no option but to decide how our country is to be run.

In the world of the *Divergent* series, the citizens of Chicago live under the faction system that divides them into Abnegation, Amity, Candor, Dauntless, Erudite and the factionless. The citizens justify the faction system on the grounds that it allows everyone to decide for themselves what sort of life they think is best. As the Abnegation leader Marcus Eaton explains at Tris's Choosing Ceremony: "Welcome to the day we honor the democratic philosophy of our ancestors, which tells us that every man has the right to choose his own way in this world."

The options are limited, though, and your choice is not to be determined by what you would enjoy, but by your political philosophy. As Marcus elaborates, old Chicago "divided into factions that sought to eradicate those qualities they believed responsible for the world's disarray." Everyone is to serve the state in accordance with their faction's specialty. Tris accepts that "The goal of my life isn't just . . . to be happy." Of course, as revealed in *Allegiant*, the people of Chicago only adopted the faction system in the first place because they were manipulated into it by the Bureau of Genetic Warfare, who aren't looking to build a perfect society at all, but to produce "Divergent" individuals. But the important thing for our purposes is that the people of Chicago believe in the system. In their view, the way their society is run is how society *should* be run.

As we know, the faction system is deeply flawed. Roth's *Divergent* series is the story of a sick society. However, one of the things that make Roth's Chicago philosophically interesting is how close her dystopian state is to one of the earliest written descriptions we have of an *ideal* society. In the fourth century B.C.E., the Greek philosopher Plato tried to work out the best way for an independent city to be organized. In his *Republic*, he describes a society governed by rationality: a society in which everyone is assigned their rightful place and duties in accordance with their nature. Comparing the two fictional societies might help us to consider how our own society should be structured.

In the wake of devastating wars, democracy was replaced in Roth's Chicago by the rule of Abnegation appointees. The population is so tightly controlled by their government that anyone whose thought processes fall outside approved archetypes is labeled "Divergent" and put to death. Plato also urges us to abandon democracy for rule by state appointees. He had seen first-hand how corrupt the democracy in his native Athens had become, and was particularly horrified at the way the people unjustly executed his teacher, the philosopher Socrates.

Plato saw the fundamental flaw of democracy being that it was ruled by people who have no particular skill in ruling. In a democracy, any ignorant fool's vote counts just as much as an informed expert's, so rather than being guided by the best opinions, democracies are guided by the prejudices of folk who have no idea what they are doing. You yourself are expected to vote on matters relating to the economy, the environment, international diplomacy and war—but how much do you really know about any of those things? Like the people of Chicago, Plato thinks that rule shouldn't be in the hands of the masses but in the hands of the most suitable people for the job. Plato wrote:

> to ensure that a [normal citizen] . . . is ruled by something similar to
> what rules the best person, we say that he ought to be the slave of that

best person. . . . It isn't to harm the slave that we say he must be ruled . . . but because it is better for everyone to be ruled by divine reason.

Faction before Blood

The reorganization of Chicago began by subverting the most fundamental social building block of all: the family. Faction loyalty is supposed to be stronger than family loyalty. The motto of Tris's Faction History textbook is "Faction before blood."

One of the reasons Tris doesn't fit in is that her first loyalty is always to her family. She narrates: "My worst fear: that my family will die, and that I will be responsible." In fact, by the end of *Divergent*, she's abandoned the whole notion of faction loyalty. Escaping from the carnage as Dauntless soldiers under the control of Erudite puppeteers start to gun down everyone in the Abnegation sector, she thinks, "I will save my family. And whatever happens after that doesn't matter."

Plato, too, wanted to abolish the family. He saw the corruption that family loyalties bred in government and wanted people to focus purely on the common good instead. Children of administrators and soldiers are taken to be raised together in government institutions and no record kept of the child's origins, "so that no parent will know his own offspring or any child his parent." To emphasize that all citizens are family, they're to address each other as "father," "mother," "sister" or "brother," a practice also recommended in the Abnegation Manifesto.

Not even people's love lives are their own business. Plato notes that owners of dogs and horses try to breed their best stock and advises that the government make sure that "the best men must have sex with the best women as frequently as possible." Tris reflects that her first kiss with Four "is the best moment of my life," but there would be no such self-indulgence in Plato's city! She'd have to hook up with Eric or Peter or Al if the state said so, with the small consolation of knowing that she doesn't have to live with them—so long as she performs her reproductive duties.

Erudite

A long time ago, Erudite pursued knowledge and ingenuity for the sake of doing good. Now they pursue knowledge and ingenuity with greedy hearts.

—Tris

Erudite was formed by people who believed that humanity's problems are mainly the result of ignorance. The faction serves society by providing scientists and teachers. Erudite accept only those who pass a minimum IQ test after rigorous study, and likewise choose their leaders by an IQ test. According to the Erudite Manifesto, intelligence is a gift that must not be used for personal gain, but "as a tool for the betterment of others." According to Erudite's leader, Jeanine Matthews, the faction is "working toward a world in which people will live in wealth, comfort and prosperity."

It all sounds terribly noble, but as Tris learns, Erudite is rotten to the core. While the whole faction system is bad, Erudite is the greatest force of evil in Chicago, plotting to take over the city and impose its values on others. Worse yet, it plans to exterminate both the Abnegation and the factionless as a "drain on resources." Why did Erudite go bad? Tris's father, Andrew Prior, claims, "Valuing knowledge above all else results in a lust for power, and that leads men into dark and empty places." But why should valuing knowledge lead to a lust for power? Andrew explains: "Human reason can excuse any evil; that is why it's so important that we don't rely on it." In his view, valuing knowledge most corrupts humans because it leads us to rely primarily on our reason, instead of our compassion, and reason can be twisted to provide justification for giving into our bad desires. He's certainly right that people will twist reason to justify doing terrible things. Every politician claims to have reason on their side, no matter how callous their policies, and many have appealed to reason to justify atrocities, from slavery to terror attacks to the Nazi death camps.

Plato also believes that humanity's problems are mainly the result of ignorance. Like the Erudite, he thinks that the least ignorant should be in charge of everyone else. It's the least ignorant, after all, who best understand the world. Just as the best person to make medical decisions is someone with a thorough training in medicine, so the best person to make political decisions is someone with a thorough training in governing, not the ignorant voter in the street. In Plato's city, positions of power are only open to members of a special ruling class who are trained to be rulers. Like members of Erudite, they must undertake a rigorous and demanding course of study over many years and prove themselves especially capable. To be a member of the ruling class requires "someone who has got a good memory, is persistent, and is in every way a lover of hard work." Like all jobs in Plato's city, ruling positions are open to women as well as men, an extremely radical idea in the fourth century B.C.E.!

Whereas Andrew believes that valuing knowledge above all else is corrupting, Plato believes that those who value knowledge above all will be the least corrupt and least corruptible members of society. After all, it is the knowledgeable who best know what's right. The mere fact that they're trained to be philosophers would ensure that they'll never be "money-loving, slavish, a boaster, or a coward . . . [or in any way] unreliable or unjust." The highest leadership positions are open only to those who achieve an understanding of moral perfection. As Plato puts it, they must be "compelled to lift up the radiant light of their souls to what itself provides light for everything . . . the good itself."

Dauntless

> I think it's important to protect people. To stand up for people . . . That's what the Dauntless are supposed to do, right?
>
> —AL

Dauntless was formed by people who believed that humanity's problems are mainly the result of cowardice. The faction supplies Chicago with "protection from threats both within and without," patrolling the fence and public areas. The Dauntless Manifesto states: "We believe in ordinary acts of bravery, in the courage that drives one person to stand up for another," "in defending those who cannot defend themselves," and that "justice is more important than peace." The Manifesto further states that Dauntless don't believe "in living comfortable lives," don't believe "that we should be allowed to stand idly by," and don't believe that "mastering violence leads to unnecessary violence."

Once again, it all sounds very noble, but the ideals don't match the reality. As Tris recognizes, the Dauntless have become corrupt and brutal. Under the original Dauntless rules, recruits fighting one another in training were allowed to surrender, but by the time Tris has to trade punches with Peter, the fights don't end until one of the combatants is incapacitated. Even Tris becomes brutalized by Dauntless culture. After defeating Molly in a fight, she continues to kick her downed opponent again and again, in the stomach, chest, and face.

Dauntless take pointless risks: leaping on and off trains high above the street, placing no guardrails over their walkways, and playing dangerous games, such as when Uriah shoots a muffin off of Marlene's head with a pellet gun. Four confirms that the Dauntless have become so reckless that not even teamwork, the foundation of military success, matters to them anymore. The Dauntless even glorify self-destruction, taking Al to be a hero for throwing himself into the chasm that runs through Dauntless headquarters. Despite the dangerous architecture of their home, the Dauntless are often drunk. Tris estimates that on initiation day, most Dauntless are sloshed by noon. Not drinking at Al's funeral is enough for Tris to be labelled a "stiff."

Like Chicago, Plato's republic is defended by a warrior class. Plato recognizes that no society can survive without a military to protect it and that no government can maintain power without military support. Like Dauntless children, children of the warrior class hone their bodies with athletic activity and their combat skills with practice. Like schoolchildren of all Chicago factions, they must also study academic subjects. Such mental discipline is considered essential to serving well in the army. As Tris points out, "What good is a prepared body if you have a scattered mind?"

Plato believes that making warriors more erudite will also make them more dauntless, for they'll better understand their duty to be courageous. Further, making them more erudite will leave them less prone to corruption. Given the nature of Dauntless training, Plato wouldn't be surprised that the Dauntless have become degenerate and brutal, embracing danger and violence. He wrote that

> those who devote themselves exclusively to physical training turn out to be more savage than they should . . . the source of the savageness is the spirited part of one's nature. Rightly nurtured, it becomes courageous, but if it's overstrained, it's likely to become hard and harsh.

In fact, warrior kids are to be educated so well that they will eventually provide society's leaders. Nobody is born into the supremely educated ruling class. Rather, new members of the ruling class are chosen from particularly promising warriors when they reach adulthood. Just as Erudite allow only the most intelligent among their ranks, only those warriors who show themselves most intelligent, most honorable, and most hard working are selected for Plato's ruling class. Subjecting future rulers to rigorous physical training as young warriors is intended to instill in them the warrior values of courage, discipline, and duty. Potential members of the ruling class must demonstrate that they are "the most stable, the most courageous, and as far as possible the most graceful . . . . a noble and tough character." Like Tris, Plato recognizes that any virtue important for one profession is likely to be important for others.

Abnegation

> When I look at the Abnegation lifestyle as an outsider, I think it's beautiful . . . when I see Caleb help strangers carry their groceries, I fall in love with this life all over again.
>
> —Tris

Abnegation was formed by people who believed that humanity's problems are mainly the result of selfishness. The faction supplies Chicago's leaders. Tris explains, "My father says that those who want power and get it live in terror of losing it. That's why we have to give power to those who do not want it." Abnegation also perform work to help the factionless, like Tris's mother Natalie, who runs a volunteer agency to provide food. Abnegation avoid luxury. Tris explains that they eat plain food because "Extravagance is considered self-indulgent and unnecessary."

Erudite accuse Abnegation of withholding luxuries like cars and fresh fruit to push their ideals of self-denial on others. They urge the abandonment of Abnegation rule and a return to democracy—at least in their public articles; privately, they are working toward Erudite rule. Peter accuses Abnegation of not even knowing how to lead society out of poverty and into prosperity. While claims of Abnegation food stockpiles are nothing but Erudite propaganda, there are genuine reasons to doubt that Abnegation treat public prosperity as an important goal. When Tris reads an Erudite plaque that boasts "KNOWL-EDGE LEADS TO PROSPERITY," she notes: "Prosperity. To me the word has a negative connotation. Abnegation uses it to describe self-indulgence."

The virtue of abnegation also lies at the heart of Plato's city. You might think that Plato is naïve for expecting his rulers and enforcers to resist the temptations that come with power. However, Plato adds an ingenious twist to his system to keep the selfish from wanting to be in government: all members of the warrior and ruler classes have to live an existence so Spartan that it makes Tris's Abnegation home look like luxury. "None of them should possess any private property beyond what is wholly necessary . . . whatever sustenance moderate and courageous warrior-athletes require . . . they'll receive by taxation on the other citizens . . . they'll have common messes and live together like soldiers in a camp."

There's little point in a leader taking bribes or a warrior shaking down the citizens for protection, if none of the leaders or warriors is allowed to own anything! Also, a lack of possessions encourages the *selflessness* with which warriors are to courageously lay down their lives for the state. Plato, like Four, appreciates that bravery can spring from taking our focus away from ourselves. As Four tells Tris:

> I have a theory that selflessness and bravery aren't all that different. All your life you've been training to forget yourself, so when you're in danger, it becomes your first instinct.

Conversely, Tris tells Four: "You can't be fearless, remember? . . . Because you still care about things. About your life."

Candor

> Truth makes us transparent. Truth makes us strong. Truth makes us inextricable.
>
> —Candor Manifesto

Candor was formed by people who believed that humanity's problems are mainly the result of dishonesty. The faction provides Chicago's lawyers—a new twist on the old profession to say the least. Like Candor, Plato sees honesty as essential for a healthy society, and as in the case of selflessness, Plato thinks the virtue of honesty is essential for everyone, rather than being the province of one class of people. Since understanding leads to good behavior, people must be educated in the truth. Lying about important matters is forbidden. For instance, nobody is allowed to tell stories about "gods warring, fighting, or plotting against one another, for they aren't true." Likewise, nobody may tell false tales of the afterlife that might make death in battle look unattractive to soldiers.

However, like Erudite, Plato didn't believe that honesty should be unrestricted when the lies come from the administration and are in the interests of the common good. For instance, he suggests that to improve public order, the citizens be told a myth that the different classes of society sprang from different kinds of metal in the ground and that a prophecy states that the city will come to ruin if ever ruled by someone from the wrong class. He even approved of turning political figures into holy figures in the interests of cementing the social order, recommending that in the case of particularly outstanding leaders, "the city will give them public memorials and sacrifices and honor them as demigods, but if not, as in any case blessed and divine."

When the Erudite attempt to seize power, they must inject the Dauntless with serum so that, as Tris puts it, "the entire faction is brain-dead, obedient, and trained to kill. Perfect soldiers." Plato proposes dispensing with the technology and securing control purely through that other popular Erudite tool: lying to the public. Amity agrees: the Amity Manifesto states that for the sake of keeping the peace, you shouldn't think negative things about people, even if the things you are thinking happen to be true! Even Abnegation is all in favor of withholding information for the common good. Caleb complains about his Abnegation upbringing: "We weren't allowed to ask questions . . . we weren't allowed to know things"

The Factionless

This is where the factionless live. Because they failed to complete initiation into whatever faction they chose, they live in poverty, doing the work no one else wants to do.

—Tris

At the bottom of Chicago society are the "factionless." Tris explains that to be left factionless is "our worst fear, greater

even than our fear of death." The factionless undertake the jobs
that nobody else wants: driving busses, cleaning up, maintaining buildings, and generally doing all the nasty, sweaty work
that keeps society running. Though classed as outsiders, the
factionless form the bulk of Chicago society. Tobias's mother
notes in *Insurgent* that her one small band of factionless is
twice the size of Dauntless. In theory, the faction system was
developed to best promote everyone's interests; but in practice,
it's left the factionless politically powerless and on the verge of
extermination at the hands of the Erudite—but who would
clean up the bodies?

Likewise, in Plato's republic, the largest proportion of the
population fall outside the specialized ruling and military
classes, and are responsible for doing everything else. They
farm, make things, build things, and generally get stuck with
the sort of work the factionless get stuck with in Chicago. They
have no political power and are lied to by the state, but are protected by law and by the warrior class from unjust or violent
treatment. Unlike the factionless, these folk would supposedly
be living the good life, precisely because wiser heads than
theirs are making their decisions for them.

Out of My Way, Stiff

So much for comparing Roth's Chicago to Plato's *Republic*. Can
any of it help us to reflect on what sort of society we should
strive for? The first thing to note is how plausible it seems that
Roth's society would fall apart—as she has it fall apart—and
how plausible it seems that Plato's society would also fall
apart. While both societies have numerous defects, the central
flaw they share is how open they are to corruption. Both societies reflect a disgust with the failings of democracy, and their
disgust is appropriate. Although the wars that preceded the
faction system are fictional, democracies have often gone to
war for bad reasons and have often fought in a cruel and brutal way. For instance, the democracy of Athens into which Plato
was born became a greedy bully among the Greek city-states,
squeezing former allies for protection money.

However, in a democracy there's at least the opportunity for
the public to replace the government when its interests aren't
being served. Tris's mother tells her: "Human beings as a whole

cannot be good for long before the bad creeps back in and poisons us again." Whether she is right about that, we're at the very least flawed; which means that any institution depending on human beings, like a government, is also going to develop flaws. If the only authority with the power to find flaws in the government is the government itself, then system-wide problems are going to be missed. The more that power is centralized, the easier it'll be for flaws to take hold.

Abnegation hasn't been ruling Chicago well because it has allowed the other factions to degenerate, and hasn't kept the people safe from the Erudite. Yet, because power is concentrated in Abnegation hands, ordinary people aren't in a position to see the failings of Abnegation security until it's too late. According to Four, Dauntless became corrupt because of a change in leaders. Since the leaders are the ultimate authority within Dauntless, such corruption was bound to happen sooner or later, because only the leaders can combat corruption. Likewise, Plato's rulers would become as unjust, simply because they have so much power and no external checks on how they use it.

Both Plato and the people of Chicago who live under the faction system are right to recognize that there's nothing magical about democracy that ensures good government. They are right to recognize that voters are plagued by vices like selfishness, ignorance, cowardice, dishonesty, and viciousness, which often lead them to be bad rulers. However, the right response isn't to find the people most lacking in those vices and concentrate power in their hands. That would only corrupt them. Rather, the right response is to do our best to avoid these vices, to be aware of our own ignorance in the face of genuine expertise, and to encourage other voters to do likewise.

Voters have grown proud, mistaking their right to an opinion for knowing what they are talking about. Voters routinely make decisions on issues such as the environment, the economy, and international politics without first working to master the facts. If experts are consulted at all, citizens often just look for commentators who tell them what they want to hear, rather than genuinely basing their opinions on credible expert opinion. If we, the voting public, want, we can easily sideline expert opinion and just pretend that the truth is whatever we decide it is. If we do, our democracy will fail, perhaps even disintegrating in an apocalyptic war, as America did in the world of the *Divergent* novels.

9
Class Warfare in Chicago

JILLIAN L. CANODE

While the *Divergent* series tells the story of Tris and her journey of identity, Veronica Roth's interweaving of various subplots enriches all three novels of the series. A particularly fascinating subplot focuses on the socio-economic classes present in the novels—though they're not explicitly labeled as classes. Because of this subplot, we can read the *Divergent* series as a kind of study in class warfare, where the factionless are the lower class, the factions constitute the middle class, and the Bureau is the upper class.

Reading the books through the framework of class allows us to investigate the effects a class system has on all parties involved: the factionless are destitute, the factions—and faction initiates—are too concerned about becoming factionless to notice that their lives aren't completely their own, and David and the other Bureau members at the compound outside the city are so self-righteous that they willingly contribute to the suffering of others in order to further their own cause.

If we look closely, *Divergent*'s faction system mirrors the class system of the United States. The members of the Bureau, who are the puppet masters of Tris's world, have real-world counterparts in the wealthy elite who, by manipulating and funding politicians, for example, distract the American people by perpetuating the possibility of unlimited upward mobility and the achievability of the "American Dream." The factionless mirror the American lower class and function as a warning to the factions—the middle class—of what happens if you don't work hard. Both the middle and lower classes are pitted against one another by those with wealth and power in order to distract them from realizing they're being manipulated. Ultimately, reading the novels as I suggest, the books, through their dismantling of the factions, reveal how destructive and inhumane the American meritocratic—merit-based—class system can be.

Invisibility of the Lower Class

In the first novel of the series, the factionless play a minor role, though their presence is palpable throughout the novel. The factionless serve as a threat, as a promise of what will happen if you fail to pass initiation, if you fail your faction, if your faction rejects you, or if you don't work hard enough to be part of that faction. Tris is reminded, time and again, that everything people do in her society is in service of their factions so that their society may flourish. The factionless are the people you cross the street to avoid; they're the people with whom you don't make eye contact. When you see them, you do as Tris does in *Divergent*—"*Duck your head and keep walking.*" The creep-factor is high when we first experience an actual factionless member, and this feeling of unease doesn't decrease significantly throughout the trilogy.

Additionally, what people know about the factionless seems to be very little. Tris doesn't really know where or how they really live. For the most part, she's only forced to think of them when she's actively confronted by their presence. Even if they aren't directly in front of her, their shadows linger. One reason the fear of the factionless is so powerful is their invisibility. It's much easier to strike fear into people if you can ensure they remain ignorant. Keeping the goings-on of the factionless unseen and unknown make it possible for the leaders of Tris's society to maintain order and dominance. So, they make becoming factionless tantamount to a death sentence; once you're one of them, you cease to exist. You don't come back from being factionless.

The factionless, then, occupy a strange state of being: they aren't allowed agency or self-identification. They're characters and caricatures created to scare. They are that which goes bump in the night. They represent ultimate failure. Hearkening back to Karl Marx (1818–1883), it used to be the ruling classes that were haunted by ghosts, but in Tris's world, the Bureau, through their embedded faction members and leaders, use the factionless to defuse any revolutionary power the middle class may have. The factionless, who should compose the revolutionary class, are instead rendered impotent by a mythos created by those in power.

It's important to understand why certain groups of people are kept out of sight; or, if they are seen, they must be seen in a certain light. It's also important to understand why there are so many people we choose to ignore. Fear guides such motivations. In the case of Tris's world, there's the fear of losing control of an already fragile social order. The way the factionless are treated is frightfully similar to how the poor are treated in the United States. In this way, the factionless represent the lower class of Tris's society. The factionless are factionless because they couldn't adapt or they didn't work hard enough. We often hear the same justifications for why the poor are poor, and "If they would just get a job and work harder, everything would be fine." This, of course, is a fiction invented to keep those in the middle class afraid of losing their position, just as faction members are terrified of becoming factionless.

The United States is a nation that doesn't like to acknowledge the existence of fixed socio-economic classes. Sure, there's unending talk about saving and strengthening the middle class, but the dialogue on class doesn't really reach past the stage of superficial mention or campaign rhetoric. Because of this insistence on ignoring class relations, the people of the US are able to perpetuate the ideology of the American Dream. It may have once been the case that if you worked hard enough, you could be successful both socially and economically, but there's evidence that this isn't true anymore. As Stephen J. McNamee and Robert K. Miller, Jr. assert in their essay, "The Meritocracy Myth," there are more factors that determine one's success than hard work alone. No matter how hard a person works, their labor does not guarantee advancement through class ranks. The limits on upward mobility are made to seem like they're wholly in the control of the individual. The truth of the matter is, though, that there's a complicated interplay of socio-economic forces at work that can help and hinder one's success.

Just like the factionless in the *Divergent* series, and especially in the first novel when they remain mysterious, the lower classes in the US are pitied, feared, and looked down upon. As Tris describes in *Divergent*, "Because they failed to complete initiation into whatever faction they chose, they live in poverty, doing the work no one else wants to do. They are janitors and construction workers and garbage collectors; they make fabric and operate trains and drive buses." Though the American Dream is about working hard to become a success, success itself is usually measured by the luxuries you can afford and the type of job you have. The expectation is that you'll work hard so you don't have to be the janitors and garbage collectors—so you can escape these jobs.

This isn't to say the factionless don't work hard. The problem is, however, that no matter how hard the factionless work, they are unable to overcome their social position. In Roth's universe, the factionless aren't allowed out of their factionlessness. Once you become factionless, there's nothing else for you. Tris is brought up to believe such a fate is worse than death, and her foray into an area of the city where the factionless keep one of their safe houses confirms her fears as she tries not to retch in the face of so much filth. In the US, though, the lower classes are encouraged to escape poverty—so much so that if they don't, they are told they deserve their destitution because they lacked the resolve to change their situation.

The Faction Middle Ground

Abnegation, Dauntless, Amity, Erudite, and Candor represent the five factions of Tris's world. Their manifestos indicate that each represents some virtue of humanity; the members of each faction belong to that faction because they have an aptitude for the types of behavior and mentality embodied within that faction. As we know, when you're sixteen you choose a new faction, or you may choose to remain in your own. The choosing is difficult for Tris, and indeed, there must be apprehension for anyone choosing, because if they're unable to pass initiation, they'll become factionless. Failing to pass initiation isn't the only way a person may become factionless, however. In a conversation with Four in *Insurgent*, Tris learns that the Dauntless practice age discrimination and/or ableism—discriminating against those who aren't able to perform certain tasks. Rather than become factionless, Four explains, most of the Dauntless members who've been ejected because of their "physical deterioration" choose death over life outside their community.

But why is death preferable to being factionless? As I explained earlier, and as Tris frequently reminds us in the *Divergent* novels, to be factionless means to be outside everything familiar and normal. To be factionless is to be "in poverty and discomfort; it is to live divorced from society, separated from the most important thing in life: community." The factions represent normal life. The members of the factions participate in community, they raise families, and they work to improve their world, no matter how small those improvements may be. Each faction has a specialty, whether it's farming, research, protection, governance, or information dispensation. Though they're divided by areas of aptitude, the factions mirror in many ways the middle class of the United States. The middle class, the most heralded and celebrated class in the U.S. because it represents the true spirit of the American Dream. It's composed of the same types of people, and the justification for their social and economic position is similar to the justifications offered in the *Divergent* series: each person has some ability for which they're well-suited, and where they end up in the socio-economic spectrum will reflect their talents and their willingness to put those talents to work.

There's more stratification within the middle class in the US than there is among the members of the factions, however. It's true that if you fail to pass initiation you will be sent to live among the factionless, but even within the factions there are better occupations than others. The stress Four places on training rankings during Tris's initiation period are evidence of this. While your rank will determine whether you are initiated into the faction, the higher your rank, in Dauntless at least, the more choices you have for which job you'll take within your faction. Roth doesn't spend a lot of time discussing factors outside of the natural aptitude for one faction or another, which affect a person's ability to perform well within his/her faction, but in the real world there are many aspects that affect where you land on the class spectrum.

Many Americans are proud to identify as being a part of the middle class, since the middle class is seen as the most hardworking, the most salt of the earth, and ultimately, the most "American." To be in the lower class is often cause for shame.

And though being wealthy is admirable, wealth carries its own stigmas, depending on how you acquired your wealth and what you do with your money. But there's little focus on how the rich become rich.

Instead, American politicians love to champion the middle class, and their rhetoric reflects time and again that the middle class is the economic space for which we should aim. In a recent tweet, President Obama said, "Everybody who works hard and takes responsibility deserves the chance to get ahead. That's what this country is built on." Assuming responsibility for yourself and working hard are the keys to upward mobility. You set your own limits for achievement. We see this sentiment reflected in the faction initiations. The middle class and the ideology behind it form the same foundational belief in the US.

Distraction and Downfall

Roth's factions are meant to be an ideal social model, with the goal of total co-operation, peace, and prosperity. You can see shades of communism in her novels, especially in the idea that people live and work in certain factions because, as Marx exclaims in his "Critique of the Gotha Program," "From each according to his ability, to each according to his needs!" I won't go so far as to say that Roth has communist leanings. Instead, I'll say that her novels promote the idea of social harmony through co-operation, charity, and empathy. But, these lofty goals are lost when Jeanine and her thirst for power leads the Erudite and Dauntless on a quest to destroy Abnegation.

While such a coup is a surprise, Roth makes us aware of tensions among the factions early on. Each faction, it seems, sees itself as the most valuable faction. This kind of infighting distracts the majority of faction members from the sinister goings-on behind the scenes. While faction members worry about who performs the best, who works the hardest for their community, which faction is the most valuable, who lives up to the faction manifestoes most genuinely, who would pass initiation, and who would become factionless, Jeanine is able to make her move.

If we map these happenings within and among the factions on to the American middle class, we'll see various important similarities. People in the middle class are constantly concerned about upward mobility. At the same time, though, they're even more worried about backsliding into poverty. In the midst of these concerns, members of the middle class are increasingly *distracted* by issues that don't necessarily have anything to do with economics. And, just as the factions allow themselves to be distracted by what are mainly petty concerns about reputation, we see the same thing happening in the US middle class. Moreover, just as the factions are led headfirst into their own demise, so too is the middle class disappearing.

Thomas Frank explains that members of the middle class are more occupied with social issues and the moral codes associated with those issues than they are about the ever widening gap between the upper and lower classes into which the middle class is falling. Furthermore, he states that "white working class voters" are "increasingly influenced by the conservative framing of electoral contests around social issues such as abortion, gun control, and family values, encouraging them to overlook (or misunderstand) their own economic interests." While the focus here is on white members of the middle class—there's no doubt that race is a key player in social and economic stratification—the majority of middle-class Americans vote not along economic lines but instead along moral lines, which don't seem to be the result of coincidence.

As the middle class becomes increasingly concerned with social issues, they overlook economic issues of grave importance. These social issues are a major focus of American politicians, as they supervene nicely on the ideals embodied by the American Dream, and it's these same politicians who rely on the nationalist rhetoric of the American Dream to get elected and stay in office. For example, the State of the Union Addresses from Jimmy Carter in 1979, Ronald Reagan in 1984, and Barack Obama in 2014 all stress that we can't be truly successful unless we assume responsibility for our lives and earn that success.

Hard work is a moral imperative; therefore we come to understand that if you aren't working hard enough, you aren't a very good person, you aren't a good American, and you probably deserve to be stuck on the lower rungs of society. People don't like to be called lazy or bad, so they'll work to get out from under such labels. Members of the middle class are so concerned with being "proper" Americans that they fail to recognize when those who hold the most social and economic power—the upper class—are exploiting them. The members of the factions are exploited, used, and distracted by the upper class as well, only where our upper class is rather visible, the upper class in Tris's world is a reality only to a chosen few who know about the Chicago experiment.

Upper Class of the Bureau

As we saw with the Occupy Movement in the US, people have grown tired of a minority of people having and controlling the majority of the nation's wealth. Theories abound about how it's possible for so few to have so much while so many have so little. No matter how the nation's wealth has amassed disproportionately, one theory many can agree with is that once people have wealth, they'll do as much as they can to hold onto it. And, judging by the various instances of corporate corruption we've seen in recent years, people want to keep their money even if they must do so by illegal or morally questionable means.

As mentioned earlier, the rhetoric of the American Dream and the propagation of the ideals embodied in the American Dream serve to distract the middle and lower classes from the truth about the distribution of income in the US. If you spin a tale long enough and to enough people, the story will eventually take on a life of its own. This is what happened with success stories of people who were able to "bootstrap" themselves into the upper class. What's so problematic about recycling the American Dream is that it places the responsibility for success and failure squarely on the shoulders of the individual outside of any social or economic context. Few like to say their success comes in large part from luck, privilege, or lots of help. Usually they'll say they are successful because they've worked as hard as possible to get where they are. The American Dream is then pushed on the lower and middle classes by those who stand to gain the most from the work those classes do: the upper class. Using the American Dream to distract the classes is a work of clever prestidigitation. The factionless are used to distract the factions; the lower class and the threat of poverty are used to distract the middle class as their sweat equity turns into capital and vanishes into the pockets of the members of the upper class.

How does all this translate to Tris's world? It's really hard to explain to people who haven't read *Allegiant*, and I keep bugging my friends to hurry up and finish the book so I can tell them about the factions and classes. But if you've read *Allegiant*, you know that there's life outside Tris's city, and it's a life unlike anything she's ever imagined. If, in the US, the upper class is composed of individuals who, for any number of reasons want to keep the system functioning as it is, and who are willing to stoop to subterfuge to make sure there is no anti-capitalist revolution, there's a group of people we meet in *Allegiant* who wish to keep the faction system operating smoothly. The group is the Bureau of Genetic Welfare, and they created Tris's entire world.

The Bureau believes that certain people are genetically pre-disposed to behave in certain ways and to have natural talents for certain occupations. In other words, where you end up is primarily determined by your biology. Indeed, David, the head scientist at the Chicago branch of the Bureau, explains that the majority of people are genetically damaged, and only the Divergent are genetically pure. Those who are pure are meant to rebuild what was once the United States. Nita, a resident of the compound where David and other scientists and non-scientists live and work, explains to Tris the division along genetic lines: "Support staff is more than just a job. Almost all of us are GDs—genetically damaged, leftovers from the failed city experiments . . . All of the scientists are GPs—genetically pure." In the compound, then, those considered genetically superior have more socially significant jobs than those who are considered damaged. This manner of thinking—that some people are naturally more inclined to be less mentally, physically, socially, and monetarily successful than others—isn't so different from the discriminatory excuses people in higher economic classes have used to justify the class system in the United States.

What's more, using a genetic justification to explain away social inequalities as the Bureau does is nothing more than a refusal to sort out social and economic disparities by way of discovering their root causes. The Bureau opts to try to undo the damage done by the historic Purity Wars by using much of the same scientific calculus that got them into a war in the first place. By creating the factions, the Bureau sets the stage for further conflict because they still believe humanity can be neatly sorted into groups based on the apparently black-and-white indicators of genetics. The US, by continuing to support a class system propped up by the illusion that merit alone will raise you up through the economic ranks, mirrors—though we all hope in a less dystopian reality—exactly what the Bureau is doing to those within and without the factions. As Tris says so well in *Allegiant*: "The reason the factions were evil is because there was no way out of them. . . . They gave us the illusion of choice without actually giving us a choice." Americans are told they have a choice when it comes to succeeding in life, but the reality for so many is that the possibility of success is only an illusion, and just getting by can be an immense struggle.

Lessons from *Divergent* Regarding Class

The resolution of the *Divergent* series is revolution and the abolition of the faction system as Tris had come to know it. The Allegiant and the factionless come to an accord so they can begin new lives out from under the Bureau and their social and genetic experimentation. While the Occupy Movement sparked conversation and debate over the class system in the US, revolution doesn't seem imminent. The conditions for the possibility of revolutionizing the system are present, and some people are frustrated with the wealth inequality overall in the US. However, the myth of the American Dream is so woven into the cultural tapestry of the United States that it's difficult for people to imagine that living well doesn't have to be a constant struggle. The *Divergent* series introduces us to a world that stands in the rubble of the former United States, where the class system as we know it has been wiped out. A new class system has arisen in its place, though, and Roth's novels documenting the maintenance of the faction system should seem hauntingly familiar to Americans.

Because we can map the factionless, the factions, and the Bureau of Tris's world onto the lower, middle, and upper classes of our own world, Roth helps us see the deceptive narrative of the American Dream. The middle and lower classes are set against one another so that those in control of the wealth and power can remain in power. The Bureau created the factions so as to work their will on those who survived the Purity Wars. As noted in *Allegiant*, the factions "are an artificial system, designed by scientists to keep us under control for as long as possible."

The class system in the US, while perhaps not designed by the rich and powerful, is certainly used by the rich and powerful to maintain their wealth and status. Tris shows us that how a person does in life has nothing to do with their genes; the working poor of the US demonstrate for us that merit alone can't do for us what we've been told for years that it can. The faction system proves to be an impossible lie to maintain; the threat of the factionless and the fear of widespread poverty lead certain factions to conquer others.

The promise of escaping the perils of the lower class, if you're willing to take responsibility for yourself as President Obama suggested, is proving, just like the faction system, to be a lie. The *Divergent* series shows us that no matter how well intentioned the lie may be, the consequences of perpetuating the lie are disastrous. If we're bothered by the corruption and lies Tris uncovers in her world, we should be outraged by what is happening in our own.[1]

---

[1] Thank you to Melanie R. Buchanan for forcing me to read the *Divergent* series, and thank you to Dr. Jason M. Buchanan for encouraging me to write this chapter.

10
Amity—Directly Democratic

TRIP McCROSSIN

"How will we conduct ourselves in this time of conflict," Johanna Reyes asks her fellow Amity, early in the *Insurgent* storyline, "as people who pursue peace?"

The conflict in question, which takes up the bulk of the earlier *Divergent* storyline, is the "faction" system's descent into civil war. One of the five factions, Erudite, has gone to war with another, Abnegation, with the unwitting help of a third, Dauntless, to wrest control of government.

The conduct in question would be to shelter Tris, Tobias, and other Abnegation and Dauntless refugees. They're in danger as a result of their partially successful effort to thwart Jeanine Matthews's initial attack. But their protection risks Amity's longstanding alliance with the other "essential" faction, Erudite.

What we know about Amity up to this point is mostly just the origin and general purpose it shares with the other factions. "Decades ago our ancestors realized," Marcus reminds those assembled for the Choosing Ceremony, "that it is not political ideology, religious belief, race, or nationalism that is to blame for a warring world," but rather "humankind's inclination toward evil, in whatever form that is." Identifying five such forms primarily, as five distinct vices, they divided society into the five factions, each devoted to eradicating one of the vices by championing the opposing virtue. And in pursuing their designated virtue, each faction suits itself to fulfill a particular role, or set of related roles in moving "toward a better society and a better world."

Within the faction system, Amity pursue the virtue of peacefulness, and so are thought to be well suited to be "understanding counselors and caretakers." Factions aren't limited to only the social role their virtue most suits them to, Marcus adds, and so the Amity are also responsible for producing all of the city's food. This is what makes Amity an essential faction. And if Amity is, then Erudite must also be. After all, Amity can achieve their "feats of agriculture" only "with the help of Erudite technology." And so we have the origin of Johanna's "How shall we conduct ourselves?" question.

As Tris ponders later on, though, Erudite is thought to be essential for additional reasons as well. Without Erudite "there would be inefficient farming," yes, but also "insufficient medical treatments, and no technological advances." What if Amity were essential in still more ways than these, even if Roth hasn't spelled this out precisely? As it turns out, it is—at least in terms of the trilogy's overall storyline. The Amity are essential, we find, not only for what they *do*, but also for how they *deliberate*—more precisely, how they deliberate *together*.

Getting Stuff Done

What ensues in response to Johanna's question—"How will we conduct ourselves in this time of conflict, as people who pursue peace?"—is Tris's and Tobias's crash course, and ours, in Amity's inner workings. In particular, as we see when "every Amity in the room turns to the person next to him or her and starts talking," we find at Amity's core a specific sort of democratic process.

Decisions in Amity are made through a process of direct democracy—rather, that is, than through some form of indirect or representational democracy. Another way to put this, in the language of the *Federalist Papers*: Amity is a democracy as opposed to a republic, in the sense that "in a democracy, the people meet and exercise the government in person; in a republic, they assemble and administer it by their representatives and agents."

With Amity at one extreme, the faction system is defined not only by a range of virtues, but also by a range of political ideologies. In the above terms, Abnegation is portrayed as a functioning republic, generally speaking. Candor and Erudite appear to have been designed along such lines as well, to the extent that they are led consensually by representatives with disproportional authority over the governed—Jack and Jeanine respectively. We know little more in detail in either case, though, except to say that however indirectly democratic Erudite was designed to be originally, Jeanine appears to have moved it considerably away from the republican ideal toward dictatorship. Dauntless, finally, is on the other end of the spectrum from Amity. It works with little, if any pretense of internal democratic structure, presenting itself shamelessly as an oligarchy, in which governing authority resides with a few, without consent on the part of the governed.

Not only is Amity, as a direct democracy, a fully legitimate alternative, it's the chosen ideology of the portion of the city's overall population whose virtue is to "pursue peace." A few things are worth noting here with regard to Amity's political process. First of all, the legitimacy of direct democracy is no small thing for readers to entertain, given that most of us hear from an early age that this or that form of indirect democracy is the only viable form of political organization.

Secondly, however remarkable the inclusion, Amity's choice of direct democracy is nonetheless not the city's choice as a whole. As Tris tells us in *Divergent*, it's Abnegation with its republican ideals which has "fulfilled our need for selfless leaders in government." This will no doubt be a comfort to fans of a republic. Still, in the face of their insistence that direct democracy is unworkable, it's remarkable to have it be the chosen ideology of a major portion of the population, governing both their internal and external relations.

Thirdly, while the idea of choosing the city's leadership from among the most selfless of its citizens naturally has much to recommend it, excluding the most peaceful among them has to give us pause. And this is surely all the more worrisome, given what we learn from Edith Prior at the end of *Allegiant,* about the war that precipitates the faction system in the first place.

Finally, and most tangibly, we have Tris's and Tobias's disagreement about the value of Amity's political process. They are both Abnegation-born Dauntless, yet they're diametrically opposed in their appraisal of the nature and wisdom of Amity's process—Tobias impressed, Tris not so much:

"How do they get anything done?" I say, as the minutes of chatter wear on.

"They don't care about efficiency," Tobias says. "They care about agreement. Watch."

Two women in yellow dresses a few feet away rise and join a trio of men. A young man shifts so that his small circle becomes a large one with the group next to him. All around the room, the smaller crowds grow and expand, and fewer and fewer voices fill the room, until there are only three or four. I can only hear pieces of what they say: "Peace—Dauntless—Erudite—safe house—involvement—"

"This is bizarre," I say.

"I think it's beautiful," he says.

I give him a look.

"What?" He laughs a little. "They each have an equal role in government; they each feel equally responsible. And it makes them care; it makes them kind. I think that's beautiful."

"I think it's unsustainable," I say. "Sure, it works for the Amity. But what happens when not everyone wants to strum banjos and grow crops? What happens when someone does something terrible and talking about it can't solve the problem?"

He shrugs. "I guess we'll find out."

To see the passage laid out here as Roth laid it out originally is to imagine how she means for us to see Tris's and Tobias's struggle—while on the surface it's a sort of playful bickering, it's nonetheless revealing. It clearly resonates, that is, with a non-fictional and very public disagreement that occurred in between the publications of *Divergent* and *Insurgent*.

In the fall and winter of 2011, the public airwaves were teeming with discord, often heated, over the nature and wisdom of Occupy Wall Street. Occupy, as it's come to be known, is a movement dedicated to exposing and struggling against government-sponsored corruption, in the financial industry and elsewhere. Of equal importance, it's dedicated to the ideal of acting only out of public and directly democratic deliberations, as a means of publicly demonstrating the viability of such political organization.

In those months between *Divergent* and *Insurgent*, it seemed everyone had an opinion about Occupy's goals and inner-workings, as events unfolded before worldwide media in New York City's Zuccotti Park, and in similar encampments far and wide. It's hard not to hear Tris's disdain for Amity's process resonate in, for example, Steven Colbert's satirical portrayal of Occupy in the October 31st, 2011, episode of *The Colbert Report*. It's just as hard not to hear Tobias's affection for it resonate in Marina Sitrin's and Dario Azzellini's more recent *They Can't Represent Us!*

Tris's and Tobias's struggle becomes all the more revealing when we set this resonance against the development and culmination of the storyline in *Insurgent* and *Allegiant*.

Strumming Banjos, Growing Crops, Saving Innocents . . .

To their surprise, the process initiated by Johanna's question leads Amity to decide ultimately to provide shelter to Tris, Tobias, and other Abnegation and Dauntless refugees. They provide it in light of the danger the refugees face in having succeeded, in part, in thwarting Erudite's initial military action. Even so, the Amity manage to maintain wartime neutrality. Amity's headquarters is designated as a "safe house" for refugees from any faction, but only as long as they keep no weaponry, engage in no physical or verbal conflict, don't discuss the war, and contribute to Amity's ongoing work routines. Even if there was any real prospect that our refugees would be able live under such restrictions, no matter what the danger, it isn't long before Erudite and Dauntless come looking for them. Consequently, they're forced to give up their hard-won protection and flee.

Amity drops out of the storyline for a time at this point, while various overlapping subplots develop. As the *Insurgent* storyline comes to a head, though, Amity re-emerges. An attack on Erudite is planned, by an alliance of Dauntless refugees and factionless. The goal is to destroy the data that allows Erudite to use simulations to control the Dauntless, and now also a portion of the Candor, to destroy Abnegation and take control of government. However worthy the goal, Erudite innocents will likely be harmed in the process, possibly in great numbers, which Tris asks Johanna to appeal to Amity to help to prevent. Again, we're presented with Amity's process, only this time with a particular dimension emphasized—the idea of direct democracy as leaderless, at least in the conventional sense of leadership.

"I know that we recognize no leader, so I have no right to address you as if that is what I am," she begins, but "I am hoping that you will forgive me, just this once, for asking if we can reconsider our previous decision to remain uninvolved." Johanna is a facilitator, in the generally accepted language of direct democracy. She's a representative, not in the sense of articulating what she believes the general will of Amity's population is—or worse should be; but in the sense that she helps it to develop and become known in a more unmediated way. The urgency of the inter-factional violence engulfing the city, though, motivates her to take a step away from merely facilitating Amity's general will, and toward molding it instead. Innocent Erudite "must be protected from needless slaughter," she implores, "if not because they are human beings, then because we cannot survive without them." "I propose," she continues, "that we enter the city as nonviolent, impartial peacekeepers in order to curb in whatever way possible the extreme violence that will undoubtedly occur. Please discuss this." At stake is a version of Tris's worry, "What happens when not everyone wants to strum banjos and grow crops . . . when someone does [or plans to do] something terrible and talking about it can't solve the problem?" The answer confirms her worst fears, but also with a surprising twist.

Amity resolves to continue to maintain neutrality, confirming Tris's earlier skepticism. Given the prospect of mass casualties, Johanna can't help but leave her faction, joining the ranks of the factionless, becoming eventually a leader of the Allegiant, and in so doing helping eventually to bring about a newfound peace. The peace she helps to broker isn't only between the warring factions, though; it's also between the Bureau of Genetic Welfare and the city.

. . . and Rebuilding Society

"The experiment is over," Tobias reports, in the final chapter of *Allegiant*. "Johanna successfully negotiated with the government," he continues, meaning here the US government officials overseeing the Bureau, "to allow the former faction members to stay in the city, provided they are self-sufficient, submit to the government's authority, and allow outsiders to come in and join them." What this authority looks like is that the Bureau, "once in charge of the experiment, will now keep order in Chicago's city limits." This makes "New" Chicago, thanks to Tris's heroic and tragically fatal effort to prevent the Bureau from resetting citizens' memories, "the only metropolitan area in the country governed by people who don't believe in genetic damage. A kind of paradise."

In the wake of all of this, Johanna finds herself among "the city's representatives in government"—the governing authority of the Bureau, under the auspices of the US government more generally. In this she's assisted by none other than our former, perhaps still loyal fan of Amity's direct democracy, Tobias.

The *Divergent* trilogy is part love story, part war chronicle, and part political intrigue—though not merely a political thriller. Were it this alone, it would thrill us with bouts of treachery, heroism, and the like, on the part of characters struggling with one another within a political system; but little, if any real doubt, would be cast on the system surviving more or less intact. Rather, the intrigue here is part of a dystopian narrative, portraying a society tragically worse than our own, in broadly political terms, but in a way that allows us to wonder what a better version of it, and by extension ours, would look like.

We're left to wonder, what will New Chicago's new government look like? Will it embody any of the spirit of the faction system? If so, will this be true of some factions more than others? Will it be true of Amity's in particular, and the preferred interpretation of democracy at its core?

Looking Back to Look Forward

"Happy Choosing Day," Christina wishes Tobias, in the final moments of *Allegiant*'s epilogue. It's been two and a half years since the six months of war, resistance, and revelation chronicled in the rest of the trilogy. Two and a half years of peace is an impressive thing, but in another sense, it's no time at all. It's little more than a quarter of the time, after all, that it took to get from the end of the Revolutionary War, in September of 1783, to the signing of the Constitution, in September of 1787, to its ratification the following June, to the submission to Congress of the Bill of Rights in September 1789, and finally to its ratification in December of 1791.

We can easily imagine, then, that while there's at least a provisional government in place in the city, with which Johanna presumably works as a representative of the Bureau and national government, city government's final form is still in flux. In this period of flux, we can imagine that throughout the city there's ongoing discussion as to what a more permanent government should look like. Given the circumstances, we can also imagine that such discussion is relatively urgent, in light of the two primary functions we conventionally associate with government—keeping the citizenry safe and secure, and maintaining in the process their individual liberties.

First, there's a rebel presence outside the city, looking forward to a return to warfare. Second, we don't know what the nature of the national government is any longer, in particular how much of the Constitution and Bill of Rights is intact. Knowing what we know about the post-Purity Wars experiment in Chicago, and that related experiments continue apace elsewhere, we can't help but conclude that significant portions of the Bill of Rights have been suspended.

Given their political and personal convictions, Johanna, Tobias, and Christina would naturally be part of such discussions. Rebels at the gates, eroded civil liberties at the national level, and only nascent ones at the city level, Johanna, Tobias, and Christina bring to the conversation a provocative set of predispositions. Two out of three are former Dauntless, and so inclined to struggle to maintain security, even if at the expense of liberty. Two out of three are Candor-born, and so inclined to value speaking one's mind, even at the expense of others' agreement or approval. Two out of three are fans of Amity-style direct democracy, even while prepared to work instead within an indirect democracy.

Now let's imagine one of their conversations in particular, pondering what New Chicago's government should look like. To this end, they wonder what lessons they might uncover by looking not only at the history of the city, and the history surrounding the Purity Wars, but the longer history that precedes them. Why not go back as far even as the First Amendment of the Bill of Rights? And there they find a provision that can't help but warm Johanna's and Christina's Candor-born hearts, that government "shall make no laws . . . abridging the freedom of speech, or of the press; or the right of the people peaceably to assemble, and to petition the government for redress of grievances." What better way to get a proper sense of the potential importance of such a provision for New Chicago than by looking to its history?

In one portion of its history, many years before the excesses of the Purity Wars, they find purity wars of a different sort, the Red Scares of the early- and mid-twentieth century. Johanna, being a representative of the government, might well have access to the Congressional Record, which might still exist even in spite of the Purity Wars. There she might uncover and bring to her conversation with Tobias and Christina a particularly eloquent bit of testimony, toward the end of the second Red Scare, by Alexander Meiklejohn. On November 14th, 1955, Meiklejohn testified to the Senate Subcommittee on Constitutional Rights, during the first session of the Eighty-fourth Congress, that the "First Amendment seems to me to be a very uncompromising statement." "It admits of no exceptions," he further clarified, but rather it "tells us that the Congress and, by implication, all other agencies of the government are denied any authority whatever to limit the political freedom of the citizens of the United States . . . declares that with respect to political belief, political discussion, political advocacy, political planning, our citizens are sovereign, and the Congress is their subordinate agent."

Such testimony would no doubt appeal to Johanna's, Tobias's, and Christina's generally uncompromising natures. Indeed, in the wake of the manipulation and violence they've suffered at the hands of the Bureau, and the supervising national government more generally, they would have to imagine it serving them well as part of the new city-wide Manifesto they're contemplating.

New Chicago, New Republic?

Meiklejohn's defense of such an uncompromising point of view is a function of how much of a fan he is, and assumes the rest of us are, of being a republic. To understand the language of the First Amendment is to "know what, as a self-governing nation, we are trying to be and to do," he insists. So, the extent to which we fail to understand the First Amendment is the extent to which "we are in grave danger of blocking our own purposes, of denying our own beliefs." Indirect democracy depends absolutely on the electorate being free and clear to choose who will represent them for whatever types and terms of office are in play—by being able at least to speak, read, and assemble freely with one another in forming our political preferences. The extent to which these freedoms are undermined by government is the extent to which it undermines our ability to be a fully-fledged electorate, and so the extent to which we slip toward at best a Dauntless-style oligarchy, at worst a Jeanine-style dictatorship. This will all resonate deeply with Johanna and Christina in particular, Candor-born and bred.

But Christina is also now Dauntless, as is Abnegation-born Tobias. So for them, questions of security are at least as important as questions of freedom, if not more so. In this way, they're likely to anticipate the following traditional two-part objection to Meiklejohn's "no exceptions" interpretation of the First Amendment. First off, citizens typically understand the job descriptions of their chosen representatives as including two fundamental duties: both to keep us safe and secure and to maintain our individual liberties. These same representatives typically understand this pair of duties as leading to a third, which is to balance liberty and security, at the expense of liberty if they deem it necessary. And, they would add, their authority trumps citizens' objections, as we gave them this authority in the first place by electing them under the above job description.

Second, when citizens object to such balancing acts, they claim we shouldn't be concerned. After all, they insist, we agree already to have our liberty constrained in all sorts of ways. We can't yell fire in a movie theater, say, or counsel murder, to invoke two conventional examples. The First Amendment doesn't protect these forms of expression, and so why should citizens worry about government constraining expression more systemically, by passing laws abridging otherwise free expression?

We can easily imagine that Christina and Tobias, security conscious as they are, and already used to giving up a variety of liberties in Dauntless, are likely moved by the above perspective—at least to a certain extent. We do well also, though, to hope that they're also moved by Meiklejohn's commonsense rebuttals nonetheless.

In the first place, yes, of course, the First Amendment can be used dangerously. Even the most cursory view of history tells us so. But this danger, whatever its type or degree, is still less dangerous than allowing government to abridge free expression. Why? Because, if indirect democracy is to remain any sort of democracy, the electorate has to be able to choose their representatives effectively. And choosing effectively depends on speaking, reading, and assembling freely.

In the second place, there's no question of justifying such abridgments in terms of the variety of ways in which expression is already constrained routinely and without controversy. The First Amendment was designed to be a political tool, to protect political expression in particular, not non-political expression, which is indeed often and un-controversially regulated. That we regulate non-political expression has little effect on our responsibilities as an electorate, but political expression is downright essential to it, and so must remain unequivocally unfettered. This is the sole purpose, then, of the First Amendment, to protect political expression in particular.

What's political expression? While there is no shortage of obvious cases of it, and no shortage of obvious cases of non-political expression, there's also no shortage of cases that fall uncomfortably in between. It's only in concluding his testimony that Meiklejohn hints at a way to think about this. Any "suppression of ideas about the common good," he says, "the First Amendment condemns with its absolute disapproval." But if we understand the expression protected by the First Amendment as political expression, and political expression as expression about, and so contributing to the common good, isn't the problem now that we must ask: how do we understand what constitutes the common good?

Here, Johanna's and Tobias's ears prick up, given their fondness for Amity's political process. How indeed can we determine the common good, they might chime in, other than through some sort of Amity-style directly democratic process! According to Meiklejohn's story, indirect democracy depends on a First Amendment closed to abridgement by government. This he defends by, among other things, distinguishing political from non-political speech. Distinguishing what counts as political speech requires that we understand what counts as the common good, which requires finally an ongoing directly democratic process of exploration.

The citizens of New Chicago are determined to be a self-governing people. This is clear. They may even decide to be so as an Amity-style direct democracy, even while set within a broadly republican political system outside the city limits. If they decide instead to be an indirect democracy, though, and decide furthermore to a healthy one, then the choice will naturally include a significant directly democratic dimension, in regular pursuit of popular consensus as to the nature of the common good.

Tobias speaks of bravery, in the wake of Tris's death, as "the work of every day, the slow walk toward a better life." As the people of New Chicago move together toward a more permanent form of self-government, a commitment to direct democracy, in either of the above scenarios, may well make for a slower walk to a better life, but it will also make for a braver one.[1]

---

[1] I would like to thank Marina Sitrin for kindly helping me to understand and appreciate the beauty of direct democracy.

11
Should We Execute the Erudite?

NICOLAS MICHAUD AND JESSICA WATKINS

Knowledge . . . It Must Not Be Wielded as a Weapon.

—Erudite Manifesto

Let's be honest: Veronica Roth, the author of *Divergent*, doesn't seem to think too highly of the Erudite.

Divergent tells us that we have to be very careful whom we trust. We have to be particularly careful of smart people who hoard knowledge for themselves. Really, in some ways, it isn't all that surprising that the Erudite are portrayed as so selfish, vicious, and dangerous. When you look around our own society, right now, we're pretty mistrustful of the well-educated. Think about how dangerous it is for a politician to come across as "too smart." It's important that they not seem separated from the average person.

We're becoming so mistrustful of education and educators that we are getting rid of tenure, putting teachers under the microscope, and demanding that they prove they meet the "right" standards—standards that focus more on basic-level skill-building than on deep and critical thinking. Why? Because we don't trust them! So it's no surprise that, in Roth's world, the Erudite are not allowed to rule, *because they can't be trusted to rule*. Smart people may just be too dangerous.

Now that isn't to say that the members of the other factions aren't smart. Tris is obviously smart, as is just about everyone else in the Dauntless faction; the difference is that the Erudite have chosen to dedicate themselves to the pursuit of knowledge.

117

We see that the knowledge they gain goes straight to their heads, and it doesn't take long for them to realize two things: 1. they have a lot of knowledge about how the city *should* be run; and 2. they have the *ability* to force others to do what they want. Pretty quickly, it's the Erudite leader, Jeanine Matthews, who decides that it's time for a change because she knows she can run the city better than Abnegation, and she knows she can force others to do what she wants!

So, to keep society safe, it may not be enough just to keep the Erudite away from political power; we might need to *eliminate* them entirely.

How Dangerous Is Knowledge?

Why did you fight with your enemy?

—Amity Manifesto

Well, the first problem is kind of personal to us. After all, pretty much everyone who is reading and writing this book would choose the Erudite faction. We're philosophers, after all. What is philosophy, other than the pursuit of knowledge? Surely, we can be trusted . . . We are nice people! You should trust us . . .

Alright, maybe philosophers are a *little* serious, but are we as dangerous as Roth seems to think? Really, the question is, "Is knowledge dangerous?" In other words, is knowledge really a destructive force, so powerful and so dangerous that it corrupts the Erudite and endangers everyone?

We've all heard that "knowledge is power." And—to be honest—that statement is a bit annoying and cliché. Obviously, knowledge isn't the same thing as power. Really, it makes more sense to say, "Knowledge is a *kind* of power." Power is usually connected to the idea of control. To have power over something means you can control it in some way—it means we can use it to *force* what we want. If we can control others, we can *force them to do our will.* And if we can control ourselves, it means that we can force ourselves to do something we don't want. Well, knowledge, sometimes, gives us the ability to control others, ourselves, and our situations. So, *sometimes*, knowledge gives us the ability to control and force others, and so sometimes knowledge can give us power. The Erudite use their knowledge to control others, and, so, in that case, their knowledge gives them power.

War can be more about knowledge than about brute force. If you know where the enemy is and they don't know where you are, you can *force* them to fight where and when you want. So Roth seems to be right—the fact that the Erudite have knowledge means that they can also use some of that knowledge to literally force other people to do what the Erudite want. Doesn't this mean that when the Erudite choose to pursue knowledge, they're also pursuing potential power? Citizens who choose the Erudite faction are the kind of people who *choose* to seek power, unlike, say, the Abnegation. Now, it might well be that even the Abnegation faction is also seeking a kind of power, the power of self-control, a power that Tris keeps saying she lacks. —But we won't dwell on their hypocrisy! We just can't trust people who want power, *Divergent* tells us; that's why power is forced on the one group that seems to want power the least . . . Abnegation. Even Marcus, the corrupt leader of Abnegation, was so contaminated specifically because he had knowledge few else had. Maybe it's the *knowledge* that made Jeanine and Marcus feel so powerful that they felt justified in their unethical treatment of other people—even entire factions or their own families!

Again, it might be the case that Roth isn't totally wrong. There's a lot of evidence that power goes to people's heads. Think about the Stanford prison experiment. In that experiment, people were given power *that they knew was fake*. One group was told that they would be pretend "prison guards" and the other group was told they would be pretend "prisoners." Everyone knew it was just a game. After just six days, the experiment had to be stopped, because the prison guards were psychologically torturing the prisoners AND the psychologist professor in charge of the experiment was starting to show symptoms himself, allowing the abuse of students! We see this happen with money, too. People who have a lot of money tend to have more ability to break the rules—they have better lawyers and better resources to get them out of trouble. They have *power*. When we ask people who have that kind of power (whether financial, or political) why they do what they do, they often answer, "It's my right." (Visit http://www.pnas.org/content/109/11/4086 for an in-depth discussion of such thinking.) There is something about having power that goes to our heads . . . just like Jeanine Matthews.

When we have power, we think we deserve it—even if we don't—because it makes us feel special.

So what we see is that, so far, Roth is scary right. Knowledge is a kind of power. The people who chose Erudite are choosing to have potential power—as knowledge. And people who have power—especially if they *want it*—often abuse that power *because they think they're special*. This sure describes Jeanine Matthews; she seems to think she's better than others. Actually, that much is obvious: you can't decide to force others to do what you want unless you really *believe* that you have the right! To her, Abnegation is run by a bunch of idiots going around bowing and barely subsisting, and the world would be better if she were in charge because she knows so much more than everyone else!

Why Knowledge Is Dangerous

So they can be made useful.

—Erudite Manifesto

Okay, so knowledge is dangerous and the people who seek it are also dangerous. But this isn't news. Plato pointed this out in his *Republic*. In it, he describes what might make the perfect city. He divided everyone into different groups depending on their abilities and personalities—sound familiar?—so that they could perform their jobs well. The big difference between his vision and *Divergent* is that Plato makes the smartest people the rulers! But, there's an important similarity . . . like Roth, Plato doesn't trust the smartest people. He thinks they have to be carefully watched and trained. There have to be limits on how long they can rule, they aren't allowed to have much money or stuff, and they basically have to be treated like they are servants of the community. All, we think, to keep that power—both knowledge and political—from going to their heads. (For a closer look at Plato, see the previous chapter of this volume.)

But knowledge isn't just dangerous because having it means you can control others, sometimes. And it isn't dangerous just because power can corrupt people. It's also something we fear for a couple of other terrifying reasons. Here's the problem: We think that Roth's fear of the Erudite and our general social fear of the Erudite isn't just because we know that their power is dangerous. It's because, whether we want to admit it or not, we're afraid of knowledge itself. In fact, in the Abrahamic belief system, the *original sin*, the thing that keeps us from glory, was *learning* about good and evil.

Think about it like this. Despite the fact that we go around saying, "Knowledge is power," and "The more you know, . . ." we aren't a society that really thinks that knowledge, by itself, is a good thing. After all, we're the same people who say, "Ignorance is bliss." There's something about knowledge that scares us. This is something most teachers, even if unknowingly, propagate. It's very common for parents to tell their children, especially when they go to college, "Don't let all that philosophy change you. Stick to your beliefs!" Ignorance—among followers—is also bliss to leaders seeking to keep their power. *Keeping* knowledge from people is a common form of social control. As the Amity are more passive when unknowingly dosed with peace serum, so are students who learn all about Dr. Martin Luther King, Jr.'s nonviolence during the US Civil Rights movement while they learn almost nothing about Malcolm X. Is it because X was a black man who believed violence was justified when fighting for freedom? Notice, however, we don't have a problem when teaching kids about George Washington's violent *fighting* for freedom—conspicuous, isn't it? Ignorance, it seems, is a tradition held in high esteem by parents and leaders because it makes life—and control—easier.

An especially scary thought comes from Michel Foucault (1926–1984), who made his career writing and thinking about power. He tells us in "Prison Talk," "It is not possible for power to be exercised without knowledge and it is impossible for knowledge not to engender power." He thought there was a direct connection between knowledge and power specifically *because it is the people in power who define knowledge.* So, Foucault thought, it isn't just that knowledge gives power or that people in power often have more knowledge they can use against others. . . . It's that what counts as knowledge is *determined* by the powerful. Powerful people get to define what we know about "right" and "wrong," for example. Wasn't it religious leaders who decided what was "wrong" for a very long time in human society? And weren't those leaders also often the people in power? Why, if not for social control, would the pre-plague

European church teach that the—oppressive—feudal system was God's plan?

Today, in the US, the most powerful people in the country define for us the meaning of the constitution (The Supreme Court), determine who's allowed to have knowledge and who isn't (Congress), and takes action against those who share knowledge the government wants kept secret (the President). In other words, don't the powerful people get to define what we know, who is allowed to know it, and punish those who share information that is restricted? Foucault pointed out that even the medical community, the community that seeks to "do no harm," defines knowledge for us. "Mental illness" is defined by the medical community. So if, for example, being gay or transgendered is defined by that community as an "illness" in their official texts—and transgendered individuals still are defined that way, then doesn't that define illness, disability, and even sexuality for us? *And* doesn't their definition act as a reason to control and treat those who are defined as "ill," even against their will?! Our ignorance of medical and psychological knowledge is useful to a community that might want to oppress or discriminate against us. Even being black was at one point officially described by the scientific and medical community as physical evidence of inferiority!

Now there's a good chance that you don't believe ignorance is a good thing. You might think that knowledge is very important. Great! But we also have to admit that our society as a whole often makes fun of the nerdy kids who pursue knowledge for knowledge's sake. Ask anyone who gets a philosophy degree; they'd all love a dollar for every time someone said to them, "What will you do with *that*?" or, "What use is philosophy?" So let's say, maybe, that we are right—that, today, we're a little off-put by knowledge for knowledge's sake. If knowledge isn't for a useful job that benefits society, we don't quite trust it . . . but why?

Upsetting Our Schemas

We believe in freedom from fear.

—Dauntless Manifesto

A psychologist named Jean Piaget (1896–1980) might have had a pretty good idea why we don't trust knowledge. He thought that beginning as kids and as we grow up, we make mental maps of the world. These maps or "schemas" weren't just maps of where things are, but also maps of facts that literally structure our brains. We don't think about them; we just make connections and store them. So when a kid looks around at the world and only sees men with short hair and women with long hair, he assumes that someone with long hair must be a woman. Of course it's really confusing for him if a person with long hair turns out to be a man, because it doesn't fit into the child's schema of how the world works.

We can imagine it like this. The people growing up in the world of *Divergent* create schemas of the way the world should be based on everything they're exposed to. They know, for example, that people who act brave and have tattoos are Dauntless. They know that people who hug a lot and wear bright clothes are Amity. They know this not just because people told it to them, but because their brains formed around their observations of the world. So when a teen changes factions, like Tris, it can be hard for her to deal with new stuff, like shaking hands and public affection. We think it should be easy to just assimilate: "I'm in a new faction; I'll just start shaking hands." But it's actually really tough, and the reason is because changing one thing in our schema usually requires changing others. You can also think of beliefs as resting on each other for stability. In the diagram below, we can see some of Tris's early beliefs. Notice how the top one comes from the belief underneath it.

When Tris realizes she's supposed to shake hands now that she's in Dauntless, she has to change a lot of other things that she knew as well—because pieces of knowledge connect and support other pieces of knowledge in our schemas. So she has to now also change what she believes about public affection. She has to question whether or not she really belongs in Dauntless. She has to question whether her father was wrong and public affection is really okay. If her father was wrong, then maybe sometimes it's okay to be selfish. If it's okay to be selfish, then everything she learned in Abnegation is wrong, and because beliefs are so interconnected you don't have to change the one at the bottom to make them all tumble down. If the top one is false, then the claim that supports it may *also* be false . . .

It's kind of like being a kid and learning Santa isn't real. . . . Now you have to question what you knew about magic, Christmas, your parents being honest—everything. In fact, you realize that the whole world is willing to conspire to lie to little kids!

Piaget calls this mess "disequilibrium." Because by the time we're teens we have a pretty good picture of the world: Dauntless are brave, Erudite are smart, Candor are honest . . . But what happens if you meet a Candor who lies? Well, if you are raised in Roth's world, that would be really disequilibrating—it would freak you out! What category should they be put in?! Your whole life, everyone fit into a category and everything you learned made sense in those categories. Now it doesn't. This is very stressful and can lead to us having to change lots of beliefs. And we *really* don't like changing our beliefs. This is, we think, why Divergent people are so dangerous to the tightly-woven social fabric of Tris's world—knowledge of their existence would shatter people's most essential rule: Faction before blood. It's societal expectation—and therefore part of *all* citizens' schemas—that everyone fits into exactly one and only *one* faction.

If *that* were untrue, imagine the disequilibrium . . . What *else* is untrue? Who *else* may break the mold? Why *can't* we belong to both faction and family? All form of social control and comfortable, familiar schemas would break down, and that may be why the Erudite leaders—remember, the people controlling knowledge and therefore holding power—don't want Divergence to enter the public schema. They're fearful of what we might learn and then have to unlearn!

Why We Fear New Knowledge

Individuals lie to themselves.

—Candor Manifesto

What we mean is this. . . . Maybe we don't like the pursuit of knowledge, especially when we're older, because it often means that we have to change the *entire way we think about the world*. One little piece of knowledge can suddenly turn everything upside down and you have to change your whole damn schema. That's why Piaget thought we often just ignore new knowledge if it requires that we change our schema—it's just easier. You see a Candor lying and you just shrug your shoulders and say, "Eh, I must have eaten a bad piece of chocolate cake," and move on—better than having to rethink the whole faction system!

There's also good reason to believe that we are especially protective of those beliefs that support the core belief that we are *special*. Consider this example: How often do you hear people arguing about gravity? Students in classrooms don't start yelling at each other about Newtonian and Einsteinian theories of gravity—well, not often. Why not? After all, gravity isn't a proven fact. Our theories about it are still theories, and science hasn't advanced enough for us to actually observe the "graviton," which is supposed to be the cause of gravity. So while we have some good theories, there's plenty of reason to question the cause and the way it works, but no one seems to get all bent out of shape over it. But evolution . . . well, that idea is one people will punch each other over. Friendships will end, students will yell at teachers, and entire countries can be divided over that theory.

What's the difference between gravity and evolution? In regards to their controversies, the main difference is that if we're wrong about gravity, it really doesn't make us any less special. But if evolution is correct, we're kind of less special— aren't we? We would just be one of many species that share common ancestry with apes. Really, it's the same reason people got all angry over the Earth-is-the-center-of-the-universe thing. If Copernicus is right, and the Earth isn't the center, we're less special!

This is all just to say that we might be scared of the Erudite not just because of how dangerous they are to us physically, but how dangerous they are to us mentally—they are disequilibrating! Imagine the risk the people of *Divergent* take, having Erudite people teach their kids! At any moment, they might start challenging the government and their parents! And that is kind of what the Erudite of *Divergent* do! Is it really wrong of them to challenge their government—well, before all the mind-controlling and killing stuff? Seriously, when they published all those obnoxious letters they weren't always entirely wrong, were they? After all, they were right that Marcus abused his son.

Are We in a Simulation?

Truth makes us inflexible.

—Alternate Translation of Candor's Manifesto

So, here's where we've gotten so far: 1. Knowledge can be dangerous because of the power it gives one person over another, and 2. Knowledge scares us because it often forces us to rethink our most deeply held beliefs. But there's one way knowledge is very dangerous, particularly to itself. Think about belief schemas: because knowledge connects to and supports other knowledge, when I learn one thing is wrong, that means I have to question other stuff. The more I learn, the more I have to question. So the act of learning is, in fact, very destructive to knowledge!

Generally, we like to think of "knowledge" as meaning "certain truth." It's something I believe, something that is true, and something I can justify as true. But that's a tough set of criteria. How do I know when my justification is good enough to believe something is true? Can I ever have enough justification? In other words, when can I say, "I know, period"? We often act like that. Jeanine sure does. She treats the knowledge she has as certain and definite truth. In that way, she's like most of us—we really like it when our knowledge is unquestionable. It can't be wrong.

But that's where things actually get dangerous. Obviously, people who believe they can't be wrong are treacherous. But even worse, it's probably impossible to ever have knowledge, if it means you have a fact that *cannot be wrong*. René Descartes—as well as many other philosophers—pointed this out. He noted that it's really hard to reach a point where we can say, "Okay. This thing—this is a certain, unquestionable, fact!" Partly, Descartes said this because he was born not long after Europe accepted that Earth was not the center of the universe and also some radical changes were taking place because of the Protestant Reformation. In other words, Descartes was growing up in the aftermath of a world that had to accept that the government, religious leaders, and institutions that seemed unquestionable actually could be wrong. This meant that there was a good chance that innocent people were persecuted, imprisoned, maybe even killed, for holding beliefs that were *right*, just because they were *divergent* from the traditional principles!

So Descartes started asking us questions that basically come to, "How do you know you aren't part of a simulation right now?" . . . Isn't it possible that we actually live in the world of *Divergent*? Hear us out, here . . . What if Roth's world actually exists, but the Erudite have created a serum that works really, *really* well. When they give it to us, we have no idea we're part of a simulation. They have released into this mass simulation Roth's books, *specifically as a way to weed out potentially divergent people*. So they watch for anyone who reads the books and then starts questioning reality. When they find those people, they, of course, kill them. The rest of us don't notice, because they just delete them from the simulation and rewrite it so that we never notice that they are gone. . . .

Okay, sure, this scenario is unlikely. But it isn't *impossible*. You might be dreaming right now. You might *think* you are reading a book, but then wake up and realize you were wrong. Really. And if you are part of a simulation, how would you check? How would you *know* you were in reality? If we are part of some evil simulation right now, *everything* we "know" is wrong. There is no USA, this book doesn't really exist, we might not even be the ages or genders we think we are! Doesn't saying that we know something require that we are certain? But we can't be certain because we don't even know if we are awake! We might all just be in a room, sitting in cold metal chairs, while hooked up to computers that monitor our progress!

This might be too much. It's true that some philosophers think we really might be part of a simulation—seriously. But a lot think that "certainty" is way too high a standard for knowledge. They think we can know things, even if it means we aren't sure we are awake right now. David Lewis (1941–2001), though, makes this whole game very interesting. He points out something that we're already realizing from Piaget: When we start investigating knowledge, we lose it. You *knew* you were reading a book until we pointed out you might actually be in a simulation. Now that you've started thinking about it, though, you aren't so sure.

Lewis thinks that epistemology—learning about knowledge—actually *destroys* our certainty. We know lots of things until we really start investigating, and then—poof!—that knowledge starts to crumble. This means that the pursuit of knowledge, itself, requires that we allow old knowledge to pass away. In particular, it requires that we be willing to let go of the need for certainty. Because, when we really examine what we know, we realize that we don't know it. We might have good evidence: "I feel myself sitting in a chair. I can see the book. I feel awake . . ." But that evidence isn't enough to say that we "know," if we are thinking about knowledge itself. You get to say you know you are reading a book when just having a friendly conversation, but you don't get to say it if you're talking about *knowledge*.

The Arrogance of Certainty

I will be my undoing if I become my obsession.

—Abnegation Manifesto

Here's the deal. It probably is true that people who have more knowledge than we do are dangerous. In fact, it's a kind of power that they can use to do us harm, and that power may well go to their heads. It's also true that knowledge scares us because it sometimes forces us to question things that we don't want to question, like, "Am I really as special as I think I am?" But, knowledge, if it's honestly pursued as knowledge, also undermines itself. The more of it you learn, the more you realize you don't know. Not just because you can see all the other stuff you still need to learn, but because you realize the stuff you *have* learned *may not be true*. You start to see how often we've been wrong. Sometimes we dream, convinced that we aren't dreaming, only to wake up later. We have, as individuals and as societies, been wrong so often that we never know, for sure, which "knowledge" is the next to topple.

Which is why we are willing to say that Roth, in a way, got something very wrong. The Erudite were never true Erudite. At least the leaders like Jeanine weren't. Like many people who learn lots, they got lazy. They became complacent and *certain* in what they knew. But it's really hard to be certain and honestly pursue new knowledge at the same time, because, as we've seen, new knowledge destroys certainty. Those "Erudite" weren't Erudite, if *Erudite* means to honestly seek knowledge, and they sure as heck weren't philosophers. The worrisome part is that, just like in the world of *Divergent*, there might be very few true seekers of knowledge left, because it always comes at a great price . . . the price of finding out, often, that you were wrong. And that's why the arrogance we find in the Erudite faction and in ourselves is the real danger.

IV

Wisdom before Faction

12
The Courage of Selflessness

DEBORAH PLESS

> Courage is not simply one of the virtues but the form of every virtue
> at the testing point, which means at the point of highest reality.
>
> —C.S. LEWIS, *The Screwtape Letters*

When Tris chose to step in front of the knife to save Albert from potential humiliation, or worse, bodily harm, she acted in a way that was simultaneously brave and selfless.

While most of the story in Veronica Roth's *Divergent* series comprises Tris's internal struggle between her two factions—Abnegation, the faction of her birth, and Dauntless, the faction of her choice—this one particular scene, coming as it does at the beginning of the story, gives us the true answer as to where Tris's allegiance lies.

This scene displays clearly that the choice between true courage and true selflessness is a false one. They are one and the same.

Why Courage and Selflessness Are the Same Thing

The reason courage and selflessness are the same isn't made explicit in the books, at least not until the final volume, and in our culture, we typically view the two concepts as being diametrically opposed.

Dauntless and Abnegation appear at first to be the most different of the factions. The Dauntless wear all black, whoop and holler as they race through the city, eat cheeseburgers and chocolate cake, and cover themselves in individualized tattoos and piercings. Meanwhile, the Abnegation wear stolid gray and pride themselves on a calm, quiet demeanor. They eat plain, simple food that's left over after the other factions have had their fill, and they shun individual expression, believing it to promote selfishness. In practice, the two factions seem to have very little in common.

Much of this can be blamed on human error. While the two factions *should* be identical ideologically speaking, they aren't, and this is largely because of the way that their leaders have chosen to enforce their philosophical ideals.

In Dauntless, the initiates are forced through a series of grueling trials, wherein the instructors insist that in order to be truly brave, you must snuff out all fear. In Abnegation, the people are forced to follow legalistic guidelines that hamper human expression, in order, we assume, to make it easier for their citizens to choose selfless actions on a daily basis.

In neither case is this ultimately helpful, because out of all of the faction values—Courage, Selflessness, Intelligence, Kindness, and Honesty—courage and selflessness are the two traits that must be *chosen* on a regular basis. It's much easier, simply from a human standpoint, to inculcate habits of kindness or intelligence or honesty, than it is to train oneself in acts of courage or selflessness.

As we will see, the line between what defines courage and what defines selflessness is so small as to be virtually invisible.

The reason for this is simple. Any properly selfless act, by which we mean an act that promotes the welfare of another without regard for your own welfare, must be brave. In order to act selflessly, you must act with courage. You must be willing to shed all notions of self-preservation and the good of your own life in order to act in favor of the good of others. Conversely, any truly courageous act—and here we mean moral courage—must be selfless. To act to save yourself, though admirable and no doubt necessary, isn't truly courageous. Courage requires that we sacrifice of ourselves, in the face of fear, so that others might prosper. In other words, selflessness. Both of these virtues are dependent on the existence of an outside party that needs help, and both of them rely on a denial of our human instinct for self-preservation.

There's another factor here, however, and that's the element of daily choice. Both courage and selflessness are not properly innate. We're not born selfless persons, nor are we born brave. Both must be chosen, and chosen regularly. A woman who has made the choice to be a selfless person must remind herself of this choice, and indeed choose it anew, every day and arguably every moment. Each time a new situation presents itself to her, she must choose again to be selfless in that moment, to deny herself the human instinct to preserve, and instead to put the fate and comfort of others before herself. To do so takes courage, as it requires her to sacrifice her wellbeing without any particular assurance that she'll be provided for.

Similarly, the man who commits himself to courage must be daily reminded of his vow, as courage must be chosen again in each situation where it is required. You don't choose moral action once, and for all time, but rather you must reaffirm a commitment to moral virtue on a moment-by-moment basis, as situations arise.

Sacrifice and Social Capital

Both courage and selflessness are virtues that lose their title as such if they are connected to any form of real social capital. By social capital, what I mean is a high social reward, either in money, status, or influence, as a result of our actions. A selfless act that then leads to social recognition and elevation is, unfortunately, made less selfless in retrospect. Similarly, a courageous act that is then publicized and leads to a monetary reward becomes a work for hire, rather than a true act of moral courage. Ultimately, however, the real issue is the intention of the actor. If the actor intends to use selfless actions in order to gain social capital, then they're not selfless. If the courageous man wishes to gain recognition through acts of courage, then he isn't truly brave.

This means that an action that has no social reward attached to it, at the time it is done, is selfless or brave. The same action, when there's now a social reward connected to it, is no longer selfless. If a woman gives her lunch to a needy person one day, expecting nothing, but then receives a gift from a friend who saw her selfless act, she can't then give her lunch a second day without the awareness that her action led to a reward. The first act is selfless, but due to the reward, the second act isn't.

If the same woman were to throw herself in front of a child in order to stop a bullet, and somehow miraculously survived, she'd be lauded and celebrated—and possibly given a form of monetary compensation for her actions. The next time, however, this unlucky woman is in such a situation, her action wouldn't *properly* be called courageous. She'd still be a good and loving person to throw herself in front of the child, but it wouldn't *properly* be called a courageous act, because she knows she would be rewarded for it. Again, it would still be amazing, and wonderful, and many other adjectives besides, but the knowledge of being rewarded makes it slightly the lesser.

This isn't an argument against rewards or against encouraging people to act in courageous or selfless ways, though they know they might be rewarded. By no means should people avoid good deeds for fear that they might be rewarded. That would make for a terrible world. But it's worth remembering that a world in which good deeds are regularly rewarded, becomes one in which good deeds are done with the understanding of a reward. Therefore, in such a world, good deeds are no longer strictly good deeds, but rather a form of beneficial transaction. This isn't a terrible thing, but it's worth noting, for it furthers our understanding of Abnegation and Erudite's criticisms of Abnegation. The selfless act that leads to a reward negates selfless action. You can't *knowingly* gain social capital from a sacrifice, for then it isn't a sacrifice at all.

Double Virtues

As I noted above, when discussing choice, I referred to the selfless actor as a woman, and the courageous one as a man. This isn't an accident, but rather a commentary on our social values as we consider these two traits. Considering that as I have shown the two virtues are essentially the same, it's interesting that each has an assigned gender value. It's assumed that all men are courageous, and all women are selfless. In fact, it even goes so far as to seem doubly virtuous when a woman presents herself as courageous and a man as selfless. We remember the names of brave women of history, as we do the selfless men whose sacrifices helped ensure our future wellbeing. The crux of this, of course, is that both the men and women in these situations were being courageous *and* selfless, and that their actions reflect that.

The *Divergent* series examines this, and subverts it, most effectively in its treatment of Tris's parents, Natalie and Andrew Prior. While Tris grew up perceiving her parents as simply perfect members of Abnegation, and uncomplicated people devoted to their simple life, she later learns that both of them are actually transfers into the Abnegation faction. Her mother transferred from Dauntless, while her father transferred from Erudite. Natalie came to Chicago as an agent for the Bureau of Genetic Welfare, where she remade herself as a Dauntless. She then gave up her ability to leave the city ever again by choosing to join Abnegation, which signified great courage and sacrifice because it required she defy her controllers outside the city and give up a life of comfort and protection. It took courage to strike out like that, and it's clear she did do so with the intent of serving others—namely, the Divergents who needed to be smuggled out of the city.

Andrew Prior chose to leave Erudite in favor of Abnegation. This constitutes more of an act of selflessness—though as noted above, they're virtually indistinguishable, as Andrew actually sacrificed social capital in order to move to a position where he could better help others.

While Natalie did tell Andrew of her past, he had no first-hand understanding or knowledge of the horrors outside Chicago's walls. With this in mind, we must question whether acting with first-hand knowledge and *still* choosing to disobey the Bureau makes Natalie's choice more sacrificial, or if the degree to which Andrew was forced to take Natalie's words on faith makes his choice more of a sacrifice. Arguments can be made in both directions, but I would say that because they made the choice together, their sacrifice is shared.

This goes against the expectation that selflessness be associated with women and courage with men. Clearly, both Natalie and Andrew, and later Tris and Four, act in courageous and selfless ways that put the needs of others over their own desires and physical wellbeing. Roth should be commended for crafting a story that challenges our gendered view of self-sacrifice.

Why It All Matters

An Erudite might say, "All of this is semantic, a rather useless distinction when it comes to real life. In our world, what does it matter that courage and selflessness are essentially the same virtue?" Well, to put it simply, it matters because if we don't recognize the inherent connection between courage and selflessness, then we fall into the same trap that destroyed Abnegation and Dauntless: by trying to enforce them independently of one another, we destroy them.

Abnegation values selflessness, yes, but it values a "selflessness" based on eternal giving, not courage. The selflessness of Abnegation consisted mostly of denying yourself things so that others might have more. Alongside that, the faction practiced a form of legalistic social order that denied individuality on the assumption that individual expression is harmful to the group. While this ideal has shades of true selflessness, it's really a perversion of it.

As C.S. Lewis writes in *Mere Christianity*, "Humility is not thinking less of yourself, but thinking of yourself less." In order to properly follow Abnegation's rules of behavior, you must actually think about yourself all the time. And the following of these rules would actually create a form of pride, rather than selfless humility, because the actor would know that they would be rewarded socially for being perceived as a selfless person.

Ironically, in their efforts to enforce a culture of selflessness, the Abnegation leaders attempt to eradicate the conditions that make selflessness possible. By creating a code of behavior, Abnegation makes selflessness into something you do because you have to, rather than because you choose to. It tries to divorce selflessness from its central component: choice.

As we've seen, the act of choosing to deny yourself is an inherent courageous act. Therefore, in trying to distance themselves from the other factions—namely Dauntless—and establish a unique identity, Abnegation only creates a weaker form of their own core value. Abnegation's selflessness is so fixated on the *appearance* of selfless behavior that they miss out on opportunities for truly courageous altruism.

Take Marcus Eaton, the symbolic representation of Abnegation's decline. While Marcus is, in the story, a very good leader and quite a capable public altruist, he fails to understand the choice aspect of selflessness, trying instead to inflict his values on his wife and son. Because he believes that selflessness can be imposed on a person, he becomes an abusive and controlling husband and father. He's a cautionary tale, because Marcus's selflessness was for public display only, and therefore not real selflessness at all. He didn't sacrifice anything by being selfless, and in fact gained social capital, meaning that he did it for selfish reasons. You cannot remove courageous self-sacrifice from selflessness—it can't be done.

On the flip side, the Dauntless leader Eric paints a stark picture of what happens when a faction devoted to protecting others—selflessly—deviates from its stated course. Eric's Dauntless initiation structure was developed to create a competitive atmosphere in which each recruit was out for themselves; not in order to inculcate in the recruits a belief that their choices have meaning, and that they're at all times to choose a more *selfless*, and therefore courageous, way of protecting the city. In so doing, he tried to create a courage that was based on the absence of fear. The trouble with this is that fear is an essential part of selfless courage. You must fear the possibility that you can't save those in need. You must be afraid of being ineffective. The reason for this is that fear connotes responsibility. You only fear something when you feel responsible for that thing.

Eric's version of courage, then, is much closer to what we would call "glory," or arguably even "cruelty." He's without a doubt cruel, but his intentions are to create a new batch of Dauntless initiates who are without fear, and also without the instinct to choose selfless courage. Selfless courage, after all, doesn't follow orders. It's a matter of personal choice in the moment, and cannot be regulated. A soldier committed to true courage, rather than glory, won't follow commands that she finds counter to the needs of those around her. A soldier committed to true courage makes a bad soldier, but a good person. The problem with Eric is that he doesn't want good people; he wants good soldiers who follow orders.

Called to Be Abnegation

While the connection between selflessness and courage is interesting, it's not obvious why such a link is necessary in our daily lives. After all, few of us find any real need to choose to selflessly risk our own lives for the greater good. If we do, it's a once-in-a-lifetime decision, as opposed to Tris's circumstances, where such situations seem to appear hourly. Why then does it matter that we understand the fundamental similarity between courage and selflessness? Because if we don't see how they are linked together, then we can't properly choose either one.

Thankfully, we live in a world very different from that of *Divergent*. Our choices are smaller—usually—and less fraught with the weight of thousands of lives. This does not, however, mean that we aren't still called to selfless, courageous behavior. We are. By virtue of our position in the world, one of immense privilege, we're called daily to sacrifice and give and put others first, *because we can*. We live in a time and place that demands and desperately needs our action. We must act selflessly, and soon, because there are many lives that depend on our actions.

For that reason, it matters greatly that we understand the correlation between selflessness and courage. Selflessness without courage is just dry legalism; it's a performance of good behavior in the hopes of a social reward. It's bringing the reusable bags to the grocery store, but only because we don't want to look irresponsible in front of the other shoppers.

Courage without selflessness is pointless action, a vain attempt to save others with the hope of a financial or social reward. It's waiting to make sure that someone is filming this on their smart phone before rushing up to stop a fight. Without each other, both selflessness and courage become cynical manipulations of public goodwill, a way for us to gain social capital without having to give or risk anything of our own. They're cheap, without sacrifice, like the pain-free tattoos available in Dauntless headquarters. But when taken together, as they're meant to be, selfless courage and courageous selflessness will change the world.

Ultimately, that's why Tris stepped in front of the target and took the knives intended for Al. Not because she believed that she was stronger or better than he was, or because she wanted to prove anything to her instructors, but because it was the right thing to do. This one action defined her character for the remainder of the series, to the extent that her final sacrifice came not as a surprise, but as an understandable extension of her character arc, and a full acceptance of the necessity of private sacrifice for public gain. To stand up to injustice is inarguably right, and to do so while sacrificing and risking—without any hope of reward—is more than just right, it is *good*.

13
Dauntless Courage

GREGORY L. BOCK AND JEFFREY L. BOCK

In the opening pages of *Divergent*, we meet Dauntless faction members for the first time, climbing higher and higher up a statue at Beatrice's school. They jump from moving trains, engage in hand-to-hand combat, and confront their worst fears in mind-altering simulations.

In the Choosing Ceremony, Beatrice (Tris) chooses Dauntless over Abnegation and Erudite, the other two factions for which she demonstrates some aptitude. Her first test as a Dauntless initiate is to hurl herself off a moving train, over a gap onto the roof of the Dauntless compound. She survives, but another initiate plummets to her death, hitting the pavement below.

Is jumping from moving trains smart? Is Dauntless the faction of the brave or the reckless? Or, is courage only courage when it's directed at something worthwhile?

Is Dauntless Reckless?

In Plato's dialogue *Laches*, Nicias and Laches are watching a Dauntless-like combat demonstration, wondering whether their boys would benefit from such training, whether learning how to fight would make them more courageous. They invite Socrates to offer his input and are quickly engaged in a philosophical discussion about the nature of courage.

Socrates asks Laches to define courage, and Laches says, "Good heavens, Socrates, there is no difficulty about that: if a man is willing to remain at his post and defend himself against

141

the enemy without running away, then you may rest assured that he is a man of courage." This is exactly what the Dauntless leader Eric thinks about courage. In the arena during hand-to-hand combat training, Eric and Four argue about the rules:

> "It ends when one of you is unable to continue," says Eric.
>
> "According to Dauntless rules," Four says, "one of you could also concede."
>
> Eric narrows his eyes at Four. "According to the *old* rules," he says. "In the *new* rules, no one concedes."
>
> "A brave man acknowledges the strength of others," Four replies.
>
> "A brave man never surrenders."

Eric thinks that brave people stand their ground, come what may, but in *Laches*, Socrates argues that people can be brave even in retreat. He describes the strategy of the Scythian cavalry of fighting while fleeing. This convinces Laches, so he attempts a better definition, proposing that courage is "a sort of endurance of the soul." But Socrates counters that a fool might have endurance that we wouldn't call *brave*, and suggests that courage must be accompanied by wisdom; otherwise, it isn't courage at all. At this point, Nicias chimes in, making a distinction between rashness and courage, explaining that a rash person "does not fear what should be feared."

Aristotle, who was Plato's student, describes the virtues in general as means between the extremes of "too much" and "too little," and the virtue of courage in particular as the mean between rashness and cowardice. Are the Dauntless rash? It would appear so because they take many foolish risks, but perhaps there's a sense in which risk-taking is good in that it's a necessary part of their training. Aristotle speaks of the process of becoming virtuous in Book II of *Nicomachean Ethics*:

> For the things we have to learn before we can do them, we learn by doing them, for example men become builders by building and lyre-players by playing the lyre; so too we become just by doing just acts, temperate by doing temperate acts, brave by doing brave acts.

In other words, young people, like Dauntless initiates, who aspire to be brave should imitate the brave people around them, but the actions of the brave-in-training will fall short of wisdom because young people lack the experience of older, wiser role models.

Tris provides a good example of someone who has become brave in the full sense through training. Not long after seeing her mother gunned down, Tris and a group that includes her father and her brother are working their way back to Dauntless headquarters. She gives them the red carpet treatment, allowing them to experience the same method of entry into the building that she enjoyed on her first visit.

> "When I tell you to jump," I say, "you jump, as far as you can."
>
> "Jump?" Caleb asks. "We're seven stories up, Tris."
>
> "Onto a roof," I add. Seeing the stunned look on his face, I say, "That's why they call it a test of bravery."
>
> Half of bravery is perspective. The first time I did this, it was one of the hardest things I had ever done. Now, preparing to jump off a moving train is nothing, because I have done more difficult things in the past few weeks than most people will in a lifetime.

Training exercises may seem pointless and reckless to young initiates, but the purpose of Dauntless training is to shape the actions and feelings of trainees so that they can overcome their fears when it matters most. Having leapt from a moving train many times before, Tris is able to do so again and lead others to do the same in order to, in this case, end the simulation that Jeanine is using to slaughter the Abnegation. Perhaps requiring trainees to jump from a train on their *first* day without instructions or safeguards is a bit extreme, but preparing soldiers for battle will naturally involve taking risks.

Is Dauntless Fearless?

Some people might be inclined to define courage as fearlessness because fear is what often gets in the way of acting courageously. In the opening pages of *Divergent*, fear is what paralyzes the Amity boy who refuses to jump from the train when Tris and other Dauntless initiates leap for the first time. However, there are several reasons to think that fearlessness is neither necessary nor sufficient for courage.

For one, the people we consider the bravest among us confess to experiencing fear. In a recent interview with Matt Lauer on NBS's *Today* show, Medal of Honor recipients confessed to feeling fear on the battlefield, but they said they ignored it and acted as if they were unafraid. On the other hand, some people are fearless because they can't comprehend real danger, which doesn't sound like bravery at all. In the movie *Forrest Gump* (1994), Forrest saves his buddies during a firefight in the Vietnam War at great risk to his own life, but it's arguable that Forrest doesn't comprehend the risks he is taking. So, it'd be odd to say he was brave.

If courage is fearlessness, then none of the heroes of *Divergent* are brave. They all have fear, as the fear landscape room shows. Four has four fears, one of them being the fear of heights, which becomes apparent as he and Tris climb the Ferris wheel in *Divergent*.

> "Are you all right, Four?"
>
> "Are you human, Tris? Being up this high . . ." He gulps for air. "It doesn't scare you at all?"
>
> I look over my shoulder at the ground. If I fall now, I will die. But I don't think I will fall. A gust of air presses against my left side, throwing my body weight to the right. I gasp and cling to the rungs, my balance shifting.

Realizing that Four is afraid of heights, Tris asks him how he can survive in Dauntless with such a fear. "'I ignore my fear,' he says. 'When I make decisions, I pretend it doesn't exist.'" She's puzzled, confused by his statement. To her "there's a difference between not being afraid and acting in spite of fear, as he does."

In Book III of the *Nicomachean Ethics*, Aristotle says that people fear different things but that some things are so scary that "every sensible man" will fear them. He says, "Now the brave man is as dauntless as man may be. Therefore, while he will fear even the things that are not beyond human strength, he will face them as he ought and as the rule directs, for honor's sake." Bravery, according to Aristotle, is fearing "the right things and from the right motive, in the right way and at the right time." He thinks that only madmen feel no fear at all. Courage, then, isn't fearlessness; it's the ability to act, as Four demonstrates, in spite of your feelings.

Is Dauntless Noble?

Aristotle explains that the ends (the goal) of courage are always good. Courage is only courage if it's used for something good. If it's used for something bad, say to rob a store or hijack an airplane, then it isn't courage, but something else. As Aristotle says in Book III of *Nicomachean Ethics*, "Courage is noble. Therefore the end also is noble; for each thing is defined by its end. Therefore it is for a noble end that the brave man endures and acts as courage directs." If Aristotle's right, then some Dauntless acts are courageous and some aren't.

Eric leads the Dauntless traitors with power and confidence. On the one hand, he puts himself in danger by fighting with his troops, which seems brave. On the other hand, his energies are directed toward the wrong ends. He is ruthless and will kill innocent Abnegation men, women, and children, even without being under a mind-control simulation. As Tris says after seeing Eric and Four argue, "I feel like I am looking at two different kinds of Dauntless—the honorable kind, and the ruthless kind." Aristotle would probably agree with Tris's estimation of Eric, but he wouldn't say that Eric has a ruthless kind of courage. He would say that Eric is ruthless, *not* courageous. Eric may have guts, for lack of a better word, but he's not brave because he isn't noble.

In *The World of Divergent: The Path to Allegiant,* The Dauntless Manifesto frames the context for Dauntless courage, shedding light on the noble ends for which the Dauntless faction exists:

> *WE BELIEVE*
>
> *that peace is hard-won, that sometimes it is necessary to fight for peace. But more than that:*
>
> *WE BELIEVE*
>
> *that justice is more important than peace.*
>
> *WE BELIEVE*
>
> *in ordinary acts of bravery, in the courage that drives one person to stand up for another.*
>
> *WE BELIEVE*
>
> *in shouting for those who can only whisper, in defending those who cannot defend themselves.*

These excerpts show that the Dauntless faction was originally designed, at least in part, for the purpose of standing up for others, that Dauntless courage is about defending the weak and powerless in society.

In *Divergent*, Tris stands up for Al during the knife-throwing training. After several rounds of throwing, Eric sends Al to the target and explains that he'll stand there while Four throws knives at him until he doesn't flinch. Tris stops them: "Any idiot can stand in front of a target . . . It doesn't prove anything except that you're bullying us. Which, as I recall, is a sign of cowardice." Eric then orders Tris to take Al's place. She complies, and trusting in Four's ability with a knife, stands still as the knives fly, only suffering a minor scratch as Four brings the knives in closer and closer. Tris's act is a paradigm instance of Dauntless values, of standing up for others.

Later in *Divergent*, Tris's mother demonstrates her courage by rescuing Tris from a flooding water tank, breaking the glass and pulling her through the corridors of the Abnegation headquarters. On the way out, they run into a group of Dauntless soldiers who are under the simulation:

> I'm going to distract them. You have to run as fast as you can."
> "No." I shake my head. "I'm not going anywhere without you."
> She smiles. "Be brave, Beatrice. I love you."
> I feel her lips on my forehead and then she runs into the middle of the street. She holds her gun above her head and fires three times into the air. The Dauntless start running.

Her mother is quickly shot down, but her sacrifice allows Tris to escape. The image of her mother's blood staining the front of her shirt will forever haunt her, but Tris has now seen the ultimate act of bravery and self-sacrifice.

In *Allegiant*, Tris escapes from the city and discovers the Bureau of Genetic Welfare, the real source of the city's problems. The book cycles into its final act as Tris takes her brother, Caleb, to a date with certain death. He's volunteered to take on the mission that would remove the memories of the people who have held the city under the veil of secrecy and seclusion. Unfortunately for Caleb, the place he will go is filled with a death serum that will surely kill him.

Caleb's act is done out of guilt, to atone for the wicked things he's done. It's not done out of sacrifice or love, but out of penitence. Tris knows this, and as they reach the final bunker, the final confrontation with the Bureau's leader, David, she forces Caleb at gunpoint to hand over the memory serum and continues the mission herself:

> When I look at him, I see the boy who held my hand in the hospital when our mother broke her wrist and told me it would be all right. I see the brother who told me to make my own choices, the night before the Choosing Ceremony. I think of all the remarkable things he is—smart and enthusiastic and observant, quiet and earnest and kind.
>
> He is a part of me, always will be, and I am a part of him, too . . . I love my brother. I love him, and he is quaking with terror at the thought of death. I love him and all I can think, all I can hear in my mind, are the words I said to him a few days ago: *I would never deliver you to your own execution.*

Caleb is terrified of death, and his sacrifice doesn't have the same meaning that Tris's would. She simply cannot send him to his death.

While Tris still holds out hope that she can survive the death serum, since she's resisted many other serums, her entrance into the weapons lab is a sacrifice of love. Like that of her mother and father, she's willing to risk death to save the ones she loves.

She does indeed survive the death serum, but she faces off against David, the mastermind of the Bureau's plot. In their discussion, David belittles her mother's sacrifice. He tells her that her mom died for no reason and that she didn't have to make that sacrifice. Tris counters:

> "My mother wasn't a fool," I say. "She just understood something you didn't. That it's not sacrifice if it's someone else's life you're giving away, it's just evil."
>
> I back up another step and say, "She taught me all about real sacrifice. That it should be done from love, not misplaced disgust for another person's genetics. That it should be done from necessity, not without exhausting all other options. That it should be done for people who need your strength because they don't have enough of their own.

That's why I need to stop you from 'sacrificing' all those people and their memories. Why I need to rid the world of you once and for all."

Then, though she's survived the death serum, lived through what would have killed anyone else, she's shot and killed by David while releasing the memory-erasing serum.

Is Dauntless Selfless?

It'd be tempting, at this point, to conclude that Dauntless courage is always other-centered, that the end toward which courage must be directed is loving self-sacrifice for the sake of another. The heroes in *Divergent* take risks for one another, as Tris does for Al and her brother; and the Dauntless Manifesto declares that bravery means standing up for those who can't stand up for themselves. This makes Dauntless sound very much like Abnegation. As Four says, "Selflessness and bravery aren't that different."

Self-sacrifice for the sake of another is certainly a good reason to be brave, perhaps the best reason, but there are other occasions for bravery as well. When Four deals with Tris's death, he faces his own personal demons and struggles with the pain of loss. He aches with his sorrows and almost takes the memory serum to forget his pain, but he realizes, thanks to Christina, that forgetting wouldn't make things easier.

> There are so many ways to be brave in this world. Sometimes bravery involves laying down your life for something bigger than yourself, or for someone else. Sometimes it involves giving up everything you have ever known, or everyone you have ever loved, for the sake of something greater.
> But sometimes it doesn't.
> Sometimes it is nothing more than gritting your teeth through pain, and the work of every day, the slow walk toward a better life.
> That is the sort of bravery I must have now.

The noble end in view here isn't self-sacrifice, but self-preservation. It has to do with perseverance and the determination to go on living. But perhaps it's a kind of other-centeredness, too, for the one who goes on living continues to engage in human relationships and contribute to the happiness of others. As

Saint Paul says in *Philippians*, "I desire to depart and be with Christ, which is better by far; but it is more necessary for you that I remain in the body."

On the other hand, maybe there's a better way to think about courage. Maybe the end of true courage is simply love, including both love for others and love for self, both self-sacrifice and self-preservation.

14
You Have to Be Good before You Can Be Smart

Gregory L. Bock and Jeffrey L. Bock

At the Choosing Ceremony in *Divergent*, Marcus explains how each of the factions were formed by its members on the belief that a certain human quality was to blame for society's problems and that the cultivation of its opposite was necessary for peace.

- **Abnegation members blame selfishness and cultivate selflessness**

- **Amity members blame aggression and cultivate peace**

- **Candor members blame duplicity and cultivate honesty**

- **Dauntless members blame cowardice and cultivate courage**, and

- **Erudite members blame ignorance and cultivate knowledge.**

Each of these seems to be a pairing of a moral vice and moral virtue, except for the Erudite pairing of ignorance and knowledge. Is ignorance a moral failing? Is knowledge morally neutral? Are there moral constraints on the pursuit of knowledge?

The Erudite and Intellectual Virtue

As Veronica Roth states in *The World of Divergent,* "The word 'erudite' focuses on knowledge rather than intelligence—intelligence being something you're born with and can't necessarily control, and knowledge being something that you acquire." It's good to be born intelligent, but if you're not, it isn't something for which you can be blamed; neither is it something that you can fix. But you can fix ignorance through learning. So, why don't more people get fixed? The fact is knowledge acquisition is hard work, and some people are simply not motivated to learn. Some people are motivated but don't know how to go about it. Other people just haven't cultivated the right habits.

A virtue is a character trait needed to live well. Courage is a virtue, and intellectual courage is a special kind of courage, a special kind of virtue. Intellectual courage involves overcoming fear for the sake of acquiring knowledge, such as the fear of testing your beliefs in a public forum. In *Divergent*, Caleb could've used a little intellectual courage in order to question the information he received from his Erudite superiors. As Tris says to Caleb, Erudite isn't Candor. "There are liars here, Caleb. There are people who are so smart they know how to manipulate you."

Some philosophers, known as 'virtue epistemologists' believe that gaining knowledge requires virtue. Without acting virtuously, you can't acquire knowledge. This claim is put forward by Linda Zagzebski in her book, *Virtues of the Mind.* She maintains that to get knowledge we have to be motivated by a desire to acquire the truth, and that takes intellectual courage. Someone with the virtue of intellectual courage is more likely to get at the truth, and this is what Caleb failed to do.

As Zabzebski sees it, acting virtuously and being virtuous are two different things. The difference is that a virtuous action can be performed by someone who is not virtuous, for instance a virtuous person in training who is not yet fully virtuous. So, Erudite initiates can act virtuously by emulating their Erudite mentors—at least mentors who are uncorrupted by greed and vanity. If only virtuous people could act virtuously, then it's doubtful the rest of us could know anything at all, according to Zabzebski's theory. But unvirtuous knowers have to act like virtuous knowers in order to acquire knowledge.

Knowledge and Social Responsibility

Other philosophers, including Lorraine Code and James Montmarquet, have made similar claims. Montmarquet says that it makes little sense to hold criminals responsible for doing things they didn't know were wrong unless, of course, they should have known. One of the reasons Adolf Hitler tried to exterminate the Jews is that he thought there was a world-wide Jewish conspiracy for world domination. Hitler should have known better.

Some types of knowledge don't seem to require any moral component. We know some things about the world just because we can see. A Dauntless initiate who sees an approaching train need not have intellectual courage to arrive at the correct belief that there's an oncoming train. She just needs to look down the tracks. If the initiate fails to see the train, it's a failure of eyesight, not a failure of morals. Perhaps there is low-end knowledge, like awareness of things we can see, which doesn't need moral virtue, while there is also high-end knowledge, like science, which does.

The Erudite Manifesto

The Erudite faction was formed for the noble goal of peace. The Erudite manifesto states:

1. **"Ignorance" is defined not as stupidity but as a lack of knowledge.**

2. **Lack of knowledge inevitably leads to lack of understanding.**

3. **Lack of understanding leads to a disconnect among people with differences.**

4. **Disconnection among people with differences leads to conflict.**

5. **Knowledge is the only logical solution to the problem of conflict.**

The Erudite manifesto recognizes the social responsibility of knowledge acquisition and promotes learning as the way to avoid conflict in a diverse society. Knowledge and understanding among people with differences is a necessary step toward resolving conflict because people tend to fear what they don't know or understand. This fear breeds distrust and dehumanization, which leads to violence and war.

The manifesto also promotes intellectual generosity; it says that knowledge should be shared: "Information must always be made available to all faction members at all times. The withholding of information is punishable by reprimand, imprisonment, and, eventually, exile." The manifesto establishes the free exchange of ideas, but only within an intellectual atmosphere that subjects all ideas to certain moral and intellectual standards. It says, "Any controversial thought or idea must be supplemented by evidence in order to reduce the potential for conflict."

This is similar to the view expressed by Austin Dacey in his book *The Secular Conscience*. Dacey says that in a pluralistic society, all views should be treated with respect, even religious ones. But to respect a point of view doesn't mean just allowing it to exist. As Dacey explains, modern-day secular liberalism has made the mistake of thinking that because matters of conscience should be free from governmental interference, they should also be free from criticism. This characteristic of secular liberalism may sound respectful to some, but it fails to take matters of conscience seriously because it doesn't treat them as if they might be true. It fails to engage them in reasoned dialogue. True respect, says Dacey, takes matters of conscience seriously enough to subject them to the norms of reason of the public square: "honesty, consistency, rationality, evidential support, feasibility, legality, morality, and revisability." Dacey explains: "Understood correctly, respect is not just compatible with criticism—it entails criticism. To respect someone we must take him seriously, and taking someone seriously sometimes means finding fault with him."

The Erudite manifesto does seem to take all points of view seriously in the sense just described, but it's unclear whether the manifesto requires dissenting voices to conform in the end. Does the faction practice tolerance toward those who hold divergent views? What if someone interprets the evidence differently than the majority or the "head lady in charge"? What if someone holds a religious belief that contradicts established science? Are these people subject to coercion by the faction or just subject to criticism? The latter is compatible with the ideals of a free democracy; the former isn't. As Martha Nussbaum says in *Liberty of Conscience*, "Conscience . . . is the dignity of the person; it is, indeed, the person himself. So: everyone has inside something infinitely precious, something that demands respect from us all, and something in regard to which we are all basically equal."

Flaws of the Manifesto

In addition to the concern about tolerance, the Erudite manifesto also has a couple of flaws. First, it establishes a curriculum for the acquisition of knowledge constituted by the following disciplines: sociology, psychology, mathematics, science, communication, and history. But notice the missing humanities: literature, art, music, philosophy, and religion. What does this say about Erudite training? Do the Erudite miss out on anything by not reading philosophy and literature?

Allan Bloom says in *The Closing of the American Mind*, "Men may live more truly and fully in reading Plato and Shakespeare than at any other time, because then they are participating in essential being and are forgetting their accidental lives."

The value of philosophy is in its ability to open the mind. When students are exposed to the ideas of great thinkers, their own ideas are challenged, and their horizons are expanded. The value of literature is in its ability to allow readers to experience a different perspective and walk in the shoes of someone else. If the Erudite curriculum omits these areas of study, then the faction as a whole will lack knowledge of the complete human experience.

Second, the manifesto sets only one criterion for choosing new leaders: an intelligence test. Do smart people necessarily make better leaders? Is intelligence alone enough to lead others? Plato proposed a social hierarchy that put philosopher kings in charge of everyone else, but even in his republic, being an expert in philosophy presupposed a certain character. Plato says that leaders—philosopher kings—should love knowledge:

Won't we also then assert that the philosopher is a desirer of wisdom, not of one part and not another, but of all of it? . . . The one who is willing to taste every kind of learning with gusto, and who approaches learning with delight, and is insatiable, we shall justly assert to be a philosopher, won't we? (*Republic*, lines 475a–c)

Jeanine Matthews, the present leader of the Erudite, is a poor example of a philosopher king, for she's driven more by the lust for power than by the love of knowledge. This is most evident in her efforts to conceal the truth about what lies outside the fence. She's willing to go as far as to slaughter the entire Abnegation faction to retain power. Plato's philosopher king, on the other hand, would unveil the truth, motivated by intellectual generosity. In Plato's famous allegory of the cave, he tells of a prisoner who has been chained in a cave his whole life, but eventually escapes and reaches the surface to behold the real world for the first time. The enlightened prisoner then returns to his fellow prisoners in the cave to tell them about his experiences and liberate them. Plato's point is that a philosopher's job is to acquire knowledge and use it for the benefit of society.

Jeanine Matthews attempts to justify her diabolical plan by saying that killing innocent people will, in fact, benefit society, but it's unclear how slaughtering a whole faction benefits anyone. This is the same kind of reasoning behind Hitler's "Final Solution," the mass extermination of the Jews. Like Hitler, Jeanine doesn't respect human life and sees no moral constraints preventing her from bringing about "the greater good." But in reality, Jeanine isn't acting for the greater good. She's only concerned with holding onto power. She only uses "the greater good" to rationalize her actions.

The Bureau of Genetic Welfare is equally responsible. The Bureau is the mysterious "monster" outside the fence that supplies Jeanine with the serums. It's the arm of the larger society tasked with running a social experiment intended to separate the factions while "genetically healed" humans emerge from each of the various sides, a needed corrective, it is said, for an earlier experiment gone wrong. As David, the leader of the Bureau, explains, "Armed with all the scientific knowledge at our government's disposal, our predecessors designed experiments to restore humanity to its genetically pure state."

Matthew, another Bureau employee, attempts to distance the Bureau from the likes of Jeanine Matthews: "Knowledge is power. Power to do evil, like Jeanine . . . or power to do good, like what we're doing. Power itself is not evil." The trouble with Matthew's statement is that he reasons the same way that Jeanine does: that the ends justify the means (consequentialism). And in both cases, the Bureau and the Erudite violate the rights of the people of Chicago to accomplish their ends.

The Bureau's experiment may have started out well enough in that the first human subjects freely entered the city to participate in the experiment, but the descendents of the first subjects (Tris and others) were unaware that they, too, were research subjects. This violates the generally accepted ethical requirement of informed consent, which requires subjects be fully-informed before agreeing to an experiment.

In addition, the Bureau allowed harm to befall its human subjects for the sake of the experiment itself. As soon as Tris realizes that David just stood by and watched her mother die, she starts trembling. She says, "My mother knew you were *watching* us at every moment . . . watching as she *died* and my father died and everyone started killing each other! And did you send in someone to help her, to help me? No! No, all you did was take notes."

The Failure of the Bureau and Erudite

Both the Bureau and the Erudite use the ends to justify the means and in doing so trample on the rights of innocent human beings. Since it's possible for the pursuit of knowledge to be so detrimental to the rights of others, the pursuit of knowledge ought to be constrained by a strong conception of human dignity. Had both groups operated in the manner suggested by virtue epistemologists, the tragedies seen throughout the *Divergent* series would have been averted.

The pursuit of knowledge is not morally neutral. Not only must the acquisition of knowledge proceed in an ethically-acceptable way, but also researchers must act in an intellectually virtuous way—in order to have any high-end knowledge at all.

15
Telling the Truth at All Costs

Cole Bowman

Be honest. Do you actually think you could make it in Candor?

Could you, unflinchingly, tell someone to their face that you detest them? Would you be able to take the Truth Serum and tell your darkest secrets to a room filled with everyone you know? Can you honestly evaluate yourself for all of your own faults? The terms of Candor membership are steep, though for many citizens of the new Chicago of *Divergent*, it's worth every ounce of effort.

Divergent is an exercise in ethics. While Aristotle, the father of virtue ethics, would encourage a synthesis of the factions— or he would say that the Divergent are the only ones with a chance of reaching moral excellence—each one follows a path toward a virtue that they consider worthy of effort. Each faction has a built-in distaste for the opposing quality of their chosen virtue. Candor is all about truth, and they find dishonesty and duplicity abhorrent. As a result, they seek honesty while eschewing any sort of deception.

Because their valuation of honesty isn't shared by everyone in the city, Candor is considered by some to be entirely *inconsequential*. Max describes it as "the only disposable faction." While under Jeannine's control, the Erudite use them as a tool to defend themselves against the Dauntless. While it's easy to see Candor as less important than the other factions, due to its apparent supporting role within the world of *Divergent*, getting rid of them would be a mistake. Not only does Candor's pursuit of truth challenge the morality of each of the other factions within the city, but it also hints at the deeper philosophical tradition by pursuing truth at all costs. This is why, despite the poor opinion that many have for the people of Candor, it's likely the most philosophically important faction.

Welcome to Merciless Mart

Merciless Mart is the home of the Candor faction and its nickname is rather justified. While Candor look upon their home with pride, those from outside of the faction tend to find the forthright honesty that is taught within, well . . . *brutal*. Within Candor, nothing other than absolute honesty is permitted, with the children even being taught by their manifesto that "withholding words is the same as lying." This is why many people from outside of the faction look at the members as being loudmouthed or rude. From within, however, the Candor value truth above all else, even—or perhaps especially—the little pieces of social courtesy that most of us expect from one another every day. Christina's mother refers to politeness as "deception in pretty packaging."

In the greater world of *Divergent* the Candor faction plays a role that occupies much of the sidelines of the plot. It's talked about very little before Tris and the remaining Dauntless find safety there while hiding from the Erudite. Even then, not much is revealed about the way that they live and how they operate. For the most part, that which makes up Candor can be garnered from their manifesto or from Christina's observations of the Candor lifestyle. They wear black and white to show their view of truth, and represent themselves with a set of scales which are set unevenly to depict the "weight of the truth." Because of their trustworthiness, Candor members play an important role politically as they're difficult to manipulate. In this way, Candor members have been integral to the turnings of the world, but their real importance may not be fully appreciated unless their honesty can be explored in a deeper context.

While Candor members are so rarely at the forefront of the action, their influence can be seen by their presence along the sidelines. If we look closely, we can see just *how much* of the periphery is populated by Candor. Tris observes a few times that *many* former Candor children pick new factions to live amongst during the Choosing Ceremony. Of the Dauntless initiates who switch factions with Tris, a number are former members of Candor. Most importantly, both Christina and Peter are previous members and both have a significant impact on Tris as she's learning the ropes not just in Dauntless, but as a person within the city.

By their very presence, Candor provide something of a baseline for honesty throughout the city. Nowhere is this more evident than by observing the dynamic between Tris and Christina. When conversing with the former Candor, Tris is especially careful not to lie to her (at least not outright), as she knows the other girl's sensitivity to it. Christina will *know* if Tris is lying. This, in turn, keeps Tris honest. Well, honest*ish*. In any case, Christina's presence reminds Tris and the others in their initiate class to be truthful. In this way—extrapolated across hundreds of potential initiates, Candor permeates through the culture of the city, putting the pursuit of truth in the peoples' minds every day.

A Bowl of Glass

Candor are devoted entirely to honesty, but in the world of *Divergent*, what does "truth" really mean?

Truth has been a hotly debated topic throughout the history of philosophy. This is a question of such great magnitude in the discipline that it draws along with it an *enormous* amount of scholarship. Thousands of years' worth of thinkers have taken on the challenge of deciding what truth means. These generations of philosophers have established working guidelines to shape a meaningful discussion of the matter of truth in our everyday lives. These same guidelines provide a structure for examining its role within the factions.

For our purposes, we'll be working with two main types of truth. The first of which is known as the "Correspondence Theory" of truth. Correspondence Theory asserts that truth relates to facts in the world. It directly references the things that *are*. While many thinkers, like Immanuel Kant himself, have sought to break this down further—almost exhaustively discussing the nature of facts and the like, we'll leave it with this definition: that which is supported by reality. It's a rather intuitive way of looking at truth itself, and is probably the way that most people habitually consider the truth. This is the truth that gnaws at Tris when she's afraid to tell Christina about Will's death.

The other concept of truth is that of an absolute—capital "T"—Truth. This is most easily understood as the underlying *idea* of truth itself. It's the kind of philosophical Truth that the greatest philosophers have sought to locate through their ruminations. It's this kind of Truth that drives the Candor deep down. It's this Truth that they speak of in their manifesto and that they represent in their black and white dress.

What's most important about either of these sorts of Truth/truth is just how it relates to the Candor faction. The big difference is this: while truth is an important aspect of the factions' day-to-day lives, Truth remains an almost unspoken, underlying principle. It's the ideal that Candor is ultimately referencing when they speak of the value of honesty. How does Candor *use* either concept of Truth/truth, then? They use both to varying degrees. "T" Truth is always present in the back of their minds as their ultimate ethical goal, while "t" truth is their mechanism for achieving it.

Black and White

While many ethicists such as Aristotle have condemned lying and deceit for millennia, other philosophers like Jeremy Bentham have spent their careers bridging the gap between the value of a well-placed lie and the moral implications of honesty. This just goes to show that it's necessary to discuss Candor's honesty from more than one perspective.

For Candor, the philosophy of Immanuel Kant provides an apt assessment of their perspective on truth. In his "Categorical Imperative," Kant asserts that truth is a "perfect duty," meaning that it's the most important function that we as free-will having, decision making, philosophy-doing people have in life. The *most important*! Because we have free will, Kant states that it's our responsibility to exercise it in a way that best reflects that which we know about reality. Think back to Correspondence Theory and you'll have a good idea of what he means. For Kant, it goes even deeper than that though. According to him, it's by authentically representing reality that free will is even *able* to exist. So, it's imperative that we express truth in all that we do. It already sounds like Kant would not only have gotten Candor in the simulation, but probably would have shot right up through the ranks of the faction.

On the other side of the issue for Kant, lying both sullies our own exercise of free will, but it also inevitably harms *others* as it would alter their own decisions. If your friend asks if she looks bad in her new dress, and you lie to her in order to spare her feelings, you've made a grave transgression against her. You made her think she looks good when she doesn't. You have prevented her from taking action to look better. With this small lie in mind, she decides to wear the dress to an important occasion and it embarrasses her. Not so nice a friend, now are you?

Like Kant, Candor stresses the cost of telling even a simple lie. In their manifesto it states:

> What has become clear is that lies are just a temporary solution to a permanent problem. Lying to spare a person's feelings, even when the truth would help them to improve, damages them in the long run. Lying to protect yourself lasts for so long before the truth emerges. Like a wild animal, the truth is too powerful to remain caged.

This mirrors Kant's own view on truth almost exactly. The Candor are concerned about truth above all else. Truth is their own "perfect duty," and it is *imperative* in order to run a perfect society according to their values. In order to more fully appreciate the starkness of this standpoint, though, it's important to know where it sits with more popular perspectives, as might be presented in the other factions of the city.

The two other schools of thought mentioned above weigh in on this subject entirely differently than does Kant. The reason why these two are of particular interest in this discussion is that they both approach the matter of honesty and truth with a different trajectory. While virtue ethicists are often on the same side as Kant, as far as the very value of honesty goes, their reason for it is entirely different. Utilitarians, however, would definitely lie if it were necessary to exercising their moral goals. So, how do they all measure up when it comes to truth?

The goal of virtue ethics is to strive for an overall well-being of spirit. Virtue ethics seeks to create the "whole package" as far as our morality is concerned. This contrasts pretty significantly to the faction system, in which people devote themselves to just *one* out of five possible virtues. For virtue ethicists the number of potential virtues is almost endless, but wisdom is considered the most important one according to Aristotle.

If you are to prescribe to virtue ethics, you should in your every action consider how doing so makes you a more complete ethical figure. Think of this as the "what would Aristotle do?" approach. The exercise of your virtues should, therefore, be your first priority. Every action that you take must be evaluated as an opportunity to become a better person overall. Virtue ethics encourages honesty, therefore, so long as it doesn't impinge upon your overarching excellence of moral character.

Utilitarianism, on the other hand, stresses that every action that an individual takes should be evaluated for its overall impact on the world. This impact should maintain one of two goals: to either maximize the overall benefit or to minimize the detriment that each decision causes. Utilitarian forefather Jeremy Bentham states this explicitly in his work *A Fragment on Government*, explaining that "it is the greatest happiness of the greatest number that is the measure of right and wrong." Each situation should then be assessed on its own merits and its various implications should be calculated individually for both who and how it impacts the world.

An easy way to view each of these schools' positions on honesty is to consider their perspective on deception. Utilitarianism offers a much more critical external view of the practice of lying as a matter of pursuing the good life, in that it questions the potential outcomes of the specific lie. This contrasts distinctly with the outcomes of a virtue ethic view of lying in which the individual is judged based on the intent of their lie rather than the content or outcome. While Kant assures us that we should look toward a universal recognition of morality, where each person acts in such a way that can be applied to every other person, utilitarians are much more situationally based.

Dishonesty Makes Evil Possible

One particularly poignant criticism of Candor's view of truth was originally posed by Benjamin Constant, who questioned Kant's unwillingness to lie even when it would be detrimental to others *not* to do so. He observed the apparent absurdity of the philosopher's thought process when it came down to either helping others or refusing to lie on their behalf. Kant, in return, wrote an essay entitled "On a Supposed Right to Lie from Philanthropy" in which he defends his position against lying in order to preserve another's life. He writes that *"one who tells a lie,* however well-disposed he may be, must be responsible for its consequences . . . for truthfulness is a duty that must be regarded as the basis of all duties." Kant doesn't stop there, though. He continues: "To be *truthful* (honest in all declarations) is therefore a sacred command of reason prescribing unconditionally, one not to be constricted by any conveniences."

A pretty heavy condemnation, indeed! But, how does it work to benefit the others involved, given Kant's own imperative? Well, let's take a look at an updated version of Constant's original critique in the shape of a thought experiment used in philosophy classes the world over to explain this very principle:

Imagine for a moment that you are a German citizen and the year is 1941. Hitler is at the height of his power and the Nazi party is actively in search of *Untermenschen*—or undesirables. These "undesirables" include Jews, Romani, Slavs, Poles, Homosexuals, and many, many others. Undesirables are condemned to death either through immediate, on the spot executions or systematic, slow exterminations delivered at work camps. While statistics are markedly against you, let's assume that you have not bought into the *Zeitgeist*—the driving spirit of the time—that has aroused within your country, and you're sympathetic to the Jewish people. This sympathy has led you to hide a few Jewish friends in your home until they can find safe passage out of the country. Then, one fine afternoon, a pair of SS police officers knock on your door. They ask if you have been harboring any Jews. Should you lie?

No! Not if you are Kant. Not even this most desperate situation would convince Kant to upend his ideal that truth is an imperative. Then again, neither would the Candor. Kant and Candor agree that, while they would take other action to assure that this wouldn't come to pass, they won't lie to save the lives of the Jews. This sounds familiar, eh? Like when the Candor refused to lie to the Erudite when the Dauntless were hiding in Merciless Mart? Kant's reasoning for his statement is that it impinges upon both our moral duty to exercise honesty in the implementation of free will and the free will of those to whom you might otherwise lie.

Again, statistics are markedly against you, but an argument *can* be made for the possibility of a positive outcome from Kant's methodology. It's entirely possible that the soldiers that have come to your door in search of Jews are secretly acting against the orders of the government and have a backchannel for helping these people to escape the cruel fate they might otherwise have to face. These soldiers, like the infamous Oskar Schindler or Raoul Wallenberg, may have contrived to facilitate your friends' escape from Nazi oppression. Kant would argue that, should you lie to these people, you risk a potentially worse fate for your friends, as you likely couldn't provide them a means of escaping Germany on your own and yourself as you have broken the law. Remember Kant's insistence about your responsibility to accept the consequences of lying? This is where they get real.

So, what would a virtue ethicist do in this situation? They would probably lie. While they would likely seek some third option to lying outright, like conveniently diverting the conversation, they would lie if they had no other choice. While honesty *is* a virtue that they seek to gain a greater hold on, there are other virtues that would be questioned should they turn over their friends to the SS. The virtues of *fortitude* and *justice* would both be slighted by that action as your failure to act bravely in the face of danger would likely lead to their wrongful deaths, respectively. You would also fail at exercising Aristotle's prime virtue—*wisdom*. Given your knowledge of the German political landscape in 1941, it would be very *un*wise to hand over Jews to the police, even knowing the possibility of their involvement in some sort of liberation front. Therefore, to act with virtuous character, one virtue—*truth*—must bow to influence of others—*fortitude, justice* and *wisdom*. What's the cost of one versus the cost of three, when building a flourishing virtuous character, after all?

Like virtue ethics, utilitarians come to a very different conclusion on our Nazi problem than does Kant. When faced with the problem of the Nazi at the door—or the Erudite at the compound, a utilitarian would undoubtedly lie in order to save the Jews hiding within. Given the parameters at hand, it's the only logical choice in order to maximize the benefit and minimize the detriment. It *saves lives*. There's no greater maximization of benefit within the Utilitarian purview except to save *more* peoples' lives.

In this sense, Amity is very similar to utilitarian ethics in their decision to lie in order to keep the peace when Tris and company are at their compound. The Erudite are at the gates and the Amity know that there are people within their buildings that would likely die at their hands should they tell them that they are there. The Amity lie in order to keep the peace and to minimize the potential suffering. As stated before, however, the Candor have a completely different perspective on this kind of ethical view, which is only further underpinned by their perpetual rivalry with Amity.

Truth Makes Us Inextricable

One clear criticism of the utilitarian view of lying is directly addressed in the Candor Manifesto. It states: "we fail to understand that [lies] do not just apply to the dynamic between ourselves and our neighbors, or ourselves and our friends. What is society but a web of individual-to-individual relationships?" This tidily illustrates the potential harm that can come from even the most well-intentioned lie. The impact of each of our actions is amplified throughout society by this dynamic web of relationships, and the true consequences for nearly any action cannot be appropriately surmised by an individual. No matter how careful the utilitarian calculations for an outcome may be, unintended consequences are *always* possible.

That being said, this web, itself must be examined. The Candor manifesto also asserts that "honesty leads to peace." This sort of paradigm, in which peace is a logical result of honesty, is only feasible should *all* of the points on the web be in collusion with one another. The manifesto goes on:

> And most of all—yes, above all else—we are free to expose our dark secrets because we know the dark secrets of our neighbors, our friends, our spouses, our children, our parents, and our enemies. We know that while we are flawed in a unique way, we are not unique because we are flawed.

If *everyone* is honest, then no one has any reason to fear the consequences of honesty, according to both Kant and the

Candor. To this effect, Kant proposed what he referred to as "The Kingdom of Ends." This theory presents a society in which all people are unified under the same guiding moral principal, and are therefore considered an *end* instead of simply a means to an end.

But this isn't the case with the society at hand. Within Candor, yes, the vast majority of people are always honest. While children are still learning the rules of honesty, they speak with candor and learn how to discern lies from the truth. But Candor does not exist within a vacuum. The other factions are free to lie as they will, which threatens the Candor truth bubble.

So, can Candor honesty extend outside of the faction? While each member of Candor has a deep knowledge of their fellow members' dark secrets, they really only share this within their own faction. Tris points out frequently that the initiates are discouraged from speaking about their old factions after they have switched. So, are Peter and Christina, former stakeholders in the Candor truth, really able to provide an honest vision of Candor? While neither can be accused of being laconic or hiding their opinions, they don't share much of anything about the life within Candor, which further cloaks it in secrecy in regard to the greater population of the city. It seems, then, that Candor is closed off to the other factions in this regard, despite the insistence in their manifesto that "withholding words is the same as lying." Perhaps this is why Christina is so quick to point out the "tells" that the others give for their dishonesty. Tris bites the inside of her cheek when she lies. Will furrows his eyebrows. Christina notices these things because she has been trained to search for clues of duplicity. Because Candor doesn't trust outsiders.

Nowhere is this more evident than when the remaining Dauntless have been brought to Merciless Mart. Jack Kang forces Tris and Tobias to take the Truth Serum once they arrive on the compound. Both admit to their darkest secrets in order to prove their innocence and remain on the Candor compound. But the reason this scene is of such great importance isn't necessarily the outcomes of the truth test, but rather that it happened in the first place. Though reluctant, both Tris and Tobias agree to take the serum and neither of them *question the reason why they should have to*. This is because, deep down, they each know that the truth leads to trust amongst the factions. Truth is the mechanism by which the factions can come together.

Uneven Scales

The most important thing we learn through Tris's observations on her trials to become Dauntless is that, rather than the members of each faction embodying their specific ideal, they're instead *striving* for this ideal. This is necessary above all else when looking critically at Candor's role in society. No one has an empty fear landscape in Dauntless. It's reasonable to conclude, then that every member of Candor has a secret or two they aren't yet willing to tell.

In this way, the Candor faction mirrors one of the major aims of early philosophy, the very act of seeking. They are each in the *pursuit* of knowledge about the ideal within their faction. They're striving for excellence within this pursuit. For each and every Candor, this is the search for Truth.

Following this, the potentially trivialized concept of truth within the factions must be examined in regards to its relationship to philosophical Truth. With this in mind, the Candor perspective gains philosophical momentum. Should the striving their faction has toward truth be considered the pursuit of the ideal of Truth, then an important distinction can be made between their perceived goals and the underlying philosophical mind. In this way Candor is a tool for seeking philosophical meaning, through its assertion of ideal, essential Truth.

That said, it's not surprising that Truth is the primary objective for a fifth of the population of the city to devote themselves to. The essence of truth's role within philosophy is both beautiful and unfortunate. Truth itself, as an absolute, is one of the central questions of philosophy and it has been since the beginning of the discipline. What's beautiful is that the questioners have continued asking, even after thousands of years of speculation. What's unfortunate about the relationship between philosophy and truth is that it has yielded few answers on the matter of an objective, absolute form.

It's no small coincidence then that Christina, the most prevalent character from the Candor faction is left standing at the end of the series. The truth of the city has brought with its revelation the death of Bravery and the destruction of Knowledge. Behind every admission during an Unveiling, there was a greater piece of truth being hidden by the very existence of the factions. The factions could never be reconciled in the face of the deception that the city was founded upon. When after all of the destruction has passed and the dust is settled, Truth is left, represented by Christina. Truth, after all, is too powerful to be contained.

So, what are your darkest secrets? Should you politely package up your own deception? Is the pursuit of Truth worth the price tag? Thank you for your honesty.

V

Know Thy Faction,
Know Thy Self

16

What Do We Really Owe Our Parents?

JOHN V. KARAVITIS

Set in the distant future, in the aftermath of a civil war, Veronica Roth's *Divergent* series is a dystopian story of an American city, Chicago, which has become an isolated and self-contained world. Chicago's residents now divide themselves into five mutually exclusive yet interdependent social groups called "factions." Each faction represents an exclusory lifestyle based on living under and defending a specific value system. An annual "Choosing Ceremony" for young adults who will turn sixteen years of age allows them to voluntarily decide which faction they'll live in for the rest of their lives.

Children begin life with membership in the faction of their birth, but the Choosing Ceremony gives them the opportunity to leave their birth faction to join another, for any reason whatsoever. As your identity in society is defined by your faction membership, a change in faction membership signals a complete break from the faction of your birth, and everyone connected to it. The decision to enter a new faction is irreversible, and the only other option is to become "factionless"—which is no option at all. Throughout the tumultuous events in the series, issues regarding the nature of the family and our relationship with our parents are intimately woven together. These issues are a source of conflict and motivation for the two main protagonists, Beatrice "Tris" Prior and Tobias "Four" Eaton. Both were born in Abnegation, and both decided to leave and join Dauntless.

To leave behind the faction and the family of your birth, and so begin a new life in another faction, raises questions about the nature of the family and whether *adult* children owe their parents any duties. The idea that adult children owe their parents duties of care, respect, gratitude, and love is known as filial piety. This idea has been held sacred in both Eastern and Western cultures, and it's been a fundamental precept of many religions. Philosophers who have thought about what adult children owe their parents have argued compellingly both for and against the existence of any such duties. The *Divergent* series presents these philosophical arguments through the thoughts and actions of its two main protagonists, Tris and Tobias. Because of their vastly different childhood experiences, they each begin their adult lives on opposite sides of this issue.

So, do we as adults owe our parents complete filial piety—allegiance? If not, do we as adults owe ourselves a complete withdrawal from our parents—divergence? Or should we occupy the middle ground, where we don't abandon our parents, yet are also not completely subservient to them—insurgence? Should we decide to occupy the middle ground, is it enough for us to rebel against the child's-eye view of our parents' authority, and instead adopt a more adult view of who they once were and now are? Both Tris and Tobias struggle with these philosophical questions throughout their adult experiences as they face the challenges of living in a world of factions, civil unrest, and revolution. Divergence, insurgence, or allegiance—which do we owe our parents?

You Can't Choose Your Parents

In cultures and religions all over the world, children are expected to owe their parents a duty of filial piety throughout their entire lives. In China, filial piety, or *xiao*, is considered to be the root of morality and justice. The individual's relationship with the community is defined by adherence to filial piety, and social harmony is the ultimate benefit.

There are references to the importance of filial piety in the writings of Confucius (551–479 B.C.E.) and Mencius (372–289 B.C.E.). The cultural importance of filial piety to the Chinese can also be seen in what happened to Buddhism when it came into China. Buddhism is an individualistic belief system which stresses individual salvation and celibacy for its monks. Individuality and celibacy are contrary to what the family represents: community and procreation. To be accepted in China, Buddhism had to present itself as not being hostile to filial piety.

Filial piety is also important to many societies and religions in Europe and the Middle East. In ancient Greece, filial piety came from *eusebeia*, the idea that you honored the gods by showing filial piety to your elders. Romans saw filial piety, *pietas erga parentes,* as the distinguishing virtue of Aeneas, the founder of Rome. Many religions hold that the earthly power of parents is either derived from or mirrored in God. Each of the three Abrahamic religions mandates filial piety. In the Old Testament, "Honor thy father and thy mother" is one of the Ten Commandments (*Exodus 20:12* and *Deuteronomy 5:16*). In the New Testament, both Jesus (*Matthew 19:19*) and Paul (*1 Timothy 5:4*) preach the importance of filial piety. Islam holds that parents have the right to be looked after by their children in old age (Qur'an XVII: 23).

Present-day Western society values individual rights and individual autonomy more than filial piety, although both legally and culturally, some degree of filial piety still exists. In America, filial responsibility laws exist in twenty-nine states. Some major American holidays directly reinforce the cultural expectation of filial piety (Mother's Day and Father's Day), whereas holidays like Thanksgiving bring family members together, both physically and sentimentally.

If You Only Get to Choose Once— Choose Wisely

Veronica Roth's world of the factions hasn't abandoned filial piety. Children are expected to follow the lifestyle of their birth faction without question, and they're still required to obey their parents. However, when children become adults, they have the right to choose the faction in which they will spend the rest of their lives. Preceded by the aptitude test, which serves only to suggest and not to dictate which faction a person is best suited for, the Choosing Ceremony confirms your faction for the rest of your life.

Everyone knows that participants in the Choosing Ceremony have the freedom to choose their adult faction. However, the hope is that adult children will choose to remain in the faction of their birth. Andrew Prior expresses great shock and disappointment when he sees both his daughter Beatrice and his son Caleb choose to leave Abnegation. He loves his children, as any parent would be expected to, but he would prefer to see them choose to remain in the faction they were born and raised in. Moreover, it's understood that once a different faction is chosen, all ties to one's childhood faction are terminated. Faction transfers aren't supposed to discuss their old faction. During the Choosing Ceremony, Tris recalls a motto from her Faction History textbook: *"Faction before blood. More than family, our factions are where we belong."* Regardless of your personal feelings, the Choosing Ceremony enforces the norm that you have no absolute duty to your parents once you become an adult.

Although factions take precedence over filial piety, it still survives. The difference is that it's only recognized within a faction. Filial piety isn't recognized across faction lines. Your faction is your true family. Membership in a community is the most important thing, as seen by the fact that to be factionless is unthinkable.

But even within a faction, there are limits to filial piety. Tris learns how much factions truly override family relationships when Tobias explains why she's never seen any old Dauntless members. "Once the Dauntless reach a certain level of physical deterioration, . . . they are asked to leave. In one way or another." In the world of factions, the individual's relationship is with the state. As with the Chinese model, social harmony within and between factions is the goal; and filial piety exists only when it serves the needs of the state. How the Dauntless treat their feeble elders is the most brutal consequence of the subservience of filial piety to the needs of the state.

I Am My Mother's Daughter—Allegiance

Tris has positive feelings in general about her upbringing. She loves both of her parents, and she's grateful for how they raised her. She feels as though she owes them everything. But she found the Abnegation lifestyle smothering. Tris accepts this self-wisdom, but it hurts. She feels guilty for wanting to leave her parents and her faction of birth. Tris knows her parents would never approve of her leaving Abnegation, but she also knows that staying, even for their sakes, would not be right. Her brother Caleb tells her that it's important to think of family, but "we must also think of ourselves." As Marcus Eaton welcomes the new initiates, he explains the philosophy behind the Choosing Ceremony: "[E]very man has the right to choose his own way in this world." The goal of your life is to find your place in the world of factions and be happy. So, your place in the world matters more than filial piety, and this greatly influences Tris's decision to leave her parents.

Yet, after the Choosing Ceremony, Tris continues to see her parents through the loving eyes of her childhood. She never stops loving her parents, even after she learns disturbing details about their pasts. Her father was born in Erudite, and was a classmate of Jeanine Matthews. When she sees the Dauntless tattoo on her mother, Tris wonders how well she really knew her. Later, as she reads her mother's journal, Tris learns that, as Natalie Wright, she was part of the outside world before entering Chicago—first in Milwaukee, then in the fringe, and then at the Bureau. If you can know so little about your parents, how can you accept being forced to owe duties of care, respect, gratitude, and love to people who are, for all intents and purposes, complete strangers?

Tris never relinquishes the love of her parents and her filial piety. She never abandons her allegiance to them. In learning about their pasts, she comes to a more mature understanding of who they were. Although she learns that she never really knew her parents, she never stops loving them, even after they are dead. Her love becomes more informed and more mature, and it guides her in times of crisis. The memories of her parents, her gratitude to them, and the lessons they taught her make Tris pull back from committing suicide at the Merciless Mart, but these same memories and gratitude also lead her to risk sacrificing her life later on. She surrenders to Jeanine Matthews at Erudite headquarters, thinking she'd honor her parents by sacrificing herself for others, just as they had. When she forcibly takes Caleb's place on the suicide mission to the Weapons Lab, she recalls her parents' sacrifice, and how she can now do the same for others. Tris remains *allegiant* to the end.

I Am My Father's Son—Divergence

Tobias's father Marcus Eaton was cruel and abusive, and he made Tobias feel worthless. Even after Tobias left Abnegation for Dauntless, in order to get away from his father, Marcus remained a part of his "fear landscape." Tobias's mother, Evelyn Johnson, abandoned both of them when he was still a young child, also because of Marcus's domestic abuse. His position regarding filial piety is clear. He owes his parents nothing!

Upon entering Dauntless, Tobias had no allegiance whatsoever to either parent. When Tobias meets his parents again, he's still angry at both. There's no relationship between him and either of them, and his behavior toward both is cold and driven purely by his self-interest. In order to stop the ridicule that he's subjected to after the Candor interrogation, Tobias attacks and beats Marcus in front of a crowd, humiliating him. As his mother is the leader of the factionless, Tobias is forced to deal with her as an equal as she maneuvers for control of Chicago. He does so at arm's length, never completely trusting her.

When Tobias eventually comes to understand his parents, it's not through the eyes of a child, but rather through the eyes of an adult. With his father, filial piety is absolutely impossible. Tobias considers his father a liar and a sociopath, and nothing that he learns from dealing with Marcus as an adult changes this opinion. Tobias believes that he can reconcile to some degree with his mother, and he finds himself desiring this outcome. At the end, he does reconcile with her, thus developing some small degree of filial piety.

Given this, the *Divergent* series is not only the story of Tris and the end of the factions. The series also shows us how Tobias's feelings and perspective about his parents evolved through his interactions with them *as an adult*. Comparing Tris with Tobias, it's Tobias who makes the greater journey of self-discovery. Tobias can achieve this self-discovery because his parents remain alive throughout the series, and he can interact with them *as an adult*. In dealing with and resolving his fear of his father and his anger toward his mother, the *Divergent* series is really just as much Tobias's coming of age story as anything else.

Reconciliation on Adult Terms—Insurgence

As writers like Norman Daniels and Jane English have suggested, the relationship children have with their parents is one of power, and this power relationship is one of asymmetry and dependence. Parents are in charge, and children are powerless to change their circumstances. As a result, children can't really know their parents—anyone, actually—until they deal with them as adults. Tris and Tobias experience this truth, for it's not until they leave Abnegation and join Dauntless that they begin to have an *adult relationship* with their respective parents, and can see their parents through adult eyes. Tris loved both of her parents, but identified with and interacted more with her mother, the adult she most wanted to be like. Tobias hated and despised both his parents, but he loathed his father more. Tobias's fear of becoming just like his father is one of the strongest driving forces in his life. Nevertheless, it's not until Tris and Tobias become adults that they become capable of accurately examining the parents they identify with most.

Daniels and English both argue that because the relationship between children and their parents is asymmetrical, children have no moral obligation to their parents. Children don't ask to be born, so they can't be responsible for carrying out any responsibilities. Parents, on the other hand, chose to have children, so the existence of children places immediate moral duties on their parents.

The most common Western view of moral obligation demands respect for individual rights and individual autonomy. It also requires the intentional consent of all parties involved in a relationship. It's well-established in Western legal systems that children do not have the capacity to provide consent—only rational adults do. Therefore, to mandate filial piety upon attaining adulthood would be to demand that adult children surrender their autonomy. We'd all be starting from an inescapable relationship of dependency that we were born into, and then forced to continue throughout our adult lives. "Because you're supposed to" is *not* a valid rational argument. A lot of things may seem natural, or "right," but "because you're supposed to" is at best a sentiment, at worst a cultural mandate. Both would deny individual autonomy.

Western society, with its emphasis on individual rights and individual autonomy, *cannot mandate* filial piety from *adult* children. The most that can be said is that there is a cultural expectation that adult children should and will care for their parents to some degree, and stay actively involved in their lives.

Western society also can't provide a rational argument that adult children *should* owe their parents filial piety. Whether an adult decides to offer his parents filial piety will depend upon social custom interacting with that individual's shared history with his parents and the immediate situation.

As for what adult children *could* owe their parents, we'd have to look to the immediate relationship that exists between them as adults. The relationship between dependent children and their parents is static, whereas relationships between independent adults are dynamic. Adult relationships evolve over time, and they can end unexpectedly. To see how relationships between adult children and their parents can arise, be maintained, and even end, we can look to one type of relationship that is defensible philosophically: friendship. And for that there's a philosopher we can look to for advice: Aristotle.

My Parents/My Friends (A Guide for Faction Members)

Whether adult children *could* owe any duties to their parents may be answered by Aristotle's analysis of friendship in the *Nicomachean Ethics*. Aristotle (384–323 B.C.E.) viewed friendship, *philia*, as the one thing that a person had to have in order to make one's life complete. But friendship isn't possible between people who aren't in some way equals. Any relationship between people who aren't equal could never be considered friendship. This includes the relationship between non-adult children and their parents.

Aristotle proposed that there are three types of friendship. The first type of friendship is based on utility. People interact with each other simply for personal gain, and are more like acquaintances than true friends. The second type of friendship is based on pleasure. Here, each individual simply enjoys the company of another like-minded individual, and continues to do so until the relationship is no longer pleasurable. Both of these types of friendship are based on the personal gain that each individual perceives accruing from the friendship. The third type of friendship is based on goodness. Here, two individuals each recognize that the other is virtuous, and they choose to interact and engage with each other in mutually satisfying activities that bring out their virtuous behavior. This third type of friendship, being based on virtue, is the only true form of friendship.

Friendship provides a model which can help us resolve the question of what duties, if any, adult children *could* owe their parents. Friendship implies choice and mutual consent. It's a relationship between two adults who are equals, and it's a relationship which lacks the dependency and power imbalance that exists between non-adult children and their parents. Friendship respects the autonomy of all parties involved. Technically, this relationship isn't filial piety, of course, but it's also neither expected nor mandated by society. For a relationship which allows you the possibility to extend a duty of care, gratitude, respect, even love, to another individual, friendship between adult children and their parents is as close as we can get to filial piety by rational argument.

Be Brave

We can never really deal with our parents until we ourselves become adults. You could argue that to truly understand our parents, we'd have to "live in their shoes," and become parents ourselves. But by the time that happens, our parents might well have begun their descent into old age, becoming physically and mentally weaker. In a close relationship between adult children and their parents, the roles of dependence and independence seen during childhood will eventually reverse. These life changes alone mean that any filial relationship will always be dynamic over the years, never static.

Filial piety mandated by society and religion comes from a time when it was advantageous for people to maintain family relationships across generations. Our modern world, with its emphasis on individual rights and individual autonomy, and supported by its technological sophistication, is completely different. Reason can offer no sound argument that filial piety must be demanded of adult children toward their parents. This may seem cruel, and a bit counterintuitive, given how most people have behaved throughout time and across cultures. But we've looked at both sides of the argument, and sentiments regarding social harmony seem to be the only support for filial piety.

You could argue that the relationship between children and parents, although not chosen by the children, nevertheless demands partiality due to its special nature. It looks like common sense to say that such relationships are morally significant, and that they have a special utility that benefits society. And there's nothing wrong with sentimental feelings for your parents and pleasant memories of your youth. But a shared past history, or the idea of an implicit promise to tend to the needs of your elderly parents due to feelings of gratitude and reciprocity, isn't sufficient to argue for filial piety.

How we relate to our parents when we become adults depends on a lot of factors. If we had a pleasant upbringing, where we got along with, respected, and loved our parents, as Tris did, then filial piety would exist to some degree, if only for gratitude and love and memory's sake. Love would lead us to willingly offer filial piety.

Love and gratitude must arise on their own, out of shared history and circumstance. If you had an abusive upbringing, as Tobias had, then there's nothing to ground any sort of filial piety. You can't force someone to care for another person, especially if that person was abusive. As we see with Tobias, a victim should never be forced to surrender their self-respect and autonomy to an oppressor. Ironically, Tobias helps bring down the system—"faction before blood"—that allowed him to break free from his father and start a new adult life.

Life has always been about getting the next generation up and running. Moral responsibility always flows from parent to child, forever, and not the other way around. A river can never flow back to its source. As adult children, any relationship we choose to have with our parents can only be the result of equals agreeing to be in a relationship. Tris's and Tobias's respective journeys of self-discovery show us how this can be done, regardless of which end of the filial piety spectrum we begin. If you can look at your parents with adult eyes and see something of value that would encourage you to maintain friendly relations with them, consider yourself fortunate. But the bottom line is that there's no sound rational argument that demands filial piety from *adult* children.

Divergence, insurgence, or allegiance—which do we owe our parents? As adults, we "owe" our parents *nothing*.

17
Waking Up Divergent

JESSICA SEYMOUR

The characters in Veronica Roth's *Divergent* series exist in a dream-world constructed by the Bureau of Genetic Welfare, but before long they have their dream-world shattered by being forcibly awakened—thanks, Tris!

Roth's story shows a variety of different characters' responses to this awakening to reality. Because each character must re-evaluate their sense of identity and purpose, Roth's narrative mirrors René Descartes's argument for why knowledge and self-awareness is the only way to avoid the deception of a dream-like, false reality.

So, why should we care?

Well, let's pretend that everything you believe is a lie. It's an illusion, concocted by an evil demon controlling your senses and keeping you locked away in a dream. It may be a pleasant dream, but it's still a lie. Doesn't a dream always feel real until you're awake? How do you know that you aren't dreaming right now? In this dream, everything you see and touch is designed to trick you. So how do you break free? What's the point in valuing anything if the values and beliefs we possess are all the result of a lie?

We define ourselves by what we value, the beliefs we hold, and the place we occupy—or believe we occupy—in the world. If we discover that the assumptions we use to inform our beliefs are wrong, if the values we're brought up to believe turn out to be false, then our sense of self-identity can be disrupted—or even destroyed!

René Descartes tries to answer the sorts of questions raised above in *Meditations on First Philosophy* (1641). He writes that the knowledge which informs our beliefs is often the result of our upbringing, and it's assumed to be true even when we have no evidence. He argues that when we *assume* that our knowledge of the world is accurate, and take our beliefs and assumptions for granted, we live a life that's no more reliable than a dream. We need to test the evidence of our senses, and acquire as much knowledge as possible in order to determine the difference between fantasy and reality. Since it's possible we could be dreaming, and an evil demon could be controlling our dreams to make sure that we believe what he wants us to believe, we must question, analyze, and strive to rule out this possibility.

In the *Divergent* series, Tris and her friends learn that their dystopian society is the result of an evil demon-esque experiment in behavior and genetics. The faction system, which is the basis of their most fundamental beliefs and their reason for existing, is part of the experiment—designed to maintain peace in their society by limiting the roles which people can occupy and the personal identities which they can embody. Everything they've been taught to value, from birth to death, is a lie. They are kept ignorant by the Bureau of Genetic Welfare, allowed only certain information about themselves and the world beyond the fence, and their ignorance keeps them under the Bureau's control. The scientists running the experiment have no personal interest in the lives and happiness of their subjects. They only care that the people within the city are kept physically healthy. They are the evil demon, and their experiment is a dream designed to deceive the population. Tris and her friends have been dreaming, and now they need to—wake up!

When the characters discover the Bureau's deception, they awaken from their dream to discover the evil demon lurking in the shadows of their knowledge of the world. The value they place in the faction system, their religion, and even their personal identities are shaken. Many of the characters, particularly those who defined themselves purely in terms of their place in the faction system, are horrified by the knowledge of where they actually fit in the world. When Tris plays the video which exposes the world beyond the fence in *Insurgent*, she's branded a traitor and forced to face a tribunal. Some people just don't want to wake up. Perhaps they're comfortable in the false reality created for them by the demon, or perhaps the thought of re-evaluating the belief system which underpins their sense of identity is so frightening that they prefer to remain ignorant, rather than face the truth.

Familiar Like a Dream

In *Meditations*, Descartes reflects on the number of falsehoods that he has believed his entire life, and how his knowledge and understanding of the world stems from these falsehoods. Essentially, Descartes tries to determine whether he can trust what he believes to be true, since his beliefs may be based on *false* information. Descartes wrote *Meditations* as a response to a rise in secularism, which he felt threatened the Christian traditions on which he had based his personal identity. In order to ensure the foundation of his personal identity, Descartes proceeds to wipe his slate of knowledge entirely clean—re-evaluating and examining every belief he holds, including the assumptions on which they're based.

During his First Meditation, Descartes realizes that he can never be sure that he's not dreaming. It's possible for his senses to be deceived into believing that a dream is actually happening, and so, dreams can be mistaken for reality. As a result of this shortcoming of the senses, he speculates that it's possible that some evil demon—not God, because God is benevolent—may have been deceiving him his entire life. To have knowledge, he needs to be sure that the demon is not tricking him, and so he begins by questioning everything that can possibly be doubted. In other words, Descartes begins testing himself to see if he's awake or merely dreaming.

Descartes uses reason to arrive at the conclusion that he has a mind, because the fact that he has thoughts requires that he have a mind to think these thoughts. So, his thinking indicates that his mind is real, at least on some level. Descartes's famous line, "I think, therefore I am," comes from the belief in his own realness, because his mind can form thoughts and feelings which are separate from the senses. The senses can be mistaken and manipulated, so they can't be trusted, but the mind necessarily exists because it has thoughts, and this truth grounds Descartes's existence and the rest of his quest to distinguish reality from fiction.

With the certainty of the existence of his mind, Descartes is now able to test his accumulated beliefs and assumptions about the world from a standpoint of certain truth. By using reason to discern fact from fiction, he can avoid the faulty assumptions and false beliefs that cause many people to exist in a dream-state of ignorance. In other words, information and knowledge allow him to stabilize his beliefs and sense of self. Proper information and rational self-awareness create an ability to correctly perceive and understand the world.

Descartes's *Meditations* help show us how assumptions shape our understanding of the world, how false assumptions can create a dream-like existence based on false beliefs, and how knowledge and self-awareness help us awake from this dream state. Unlike Descartes, the characters in the *Divergent* series don't set out to have their dream-world shattered; instead, they're forcibly awakened by Tris Prior's actions and the social turmoil of their community. Once they discover the evil demon lurking in the shadows of their dreams, the characters must determine how they will respond, whether they will go back to sleep, create a new dream, or awaken to the realities of their existence.

Back to the Dream

Divergent approaches the construction of a personal identity as crucial to the happiness of the characters. Recognition that the characters have a place to belong, and that they know who they are, is deeply important to them. The faction system offers a place for most of these characters to belong. During *Allegiant*, some characters learn the Bureau used genetics to ensure that the population remained stable and easily controlled, and as a result, their self-constructed identities are meaningless side-effects of their genetics. This discovery forces the characters to question everything they thought they knew about themselves. As Cara explains to Tris in *Allegiant*: "It's the only thing I am. Erudite. And now they've told me that's the result of some kind of flaw in my genetics . . . and that the factions themselves are just a mental prison to keep us under control . . . Why bother to come out here?" In some cases, the re-evaluation of their beliefs proves too painful for the characters, and so they choose to throw themselves back onto the mercy of the evil demon.

Tobias Eaton is a Divergent character. He's not as deeply invested in the faction system as other characters, but he does recognize its value and how it shaped his own personality. For him, the faction system represents his own power to escape the physical abuse of his father. His Divergence is a source of great comfort to him because it represents his power to choose an alternative faction. When Tobias's genes are properly tested in *Allegiant*, and he discovers his reality to be a lie—that he's not truly Divergent, he responds with the same flustered loss of identity that the non-Divergent characters showed when they learn that their factions are a lie. Tobias defined his personal identity by his Divergence, and in losing this self-perception he quickly attempts to redefine himself.

When the sleeper likes the Cartesian dream more than reality, they may conspire with the evil demon to prolong the slumber. Tobias, fearing his own inadequacy once his personal identity as Divergent is proven false, chooses to latch onto the first "cause" which his new identity fits into: the Genetically Damaged vendetta, led by Nita, a fellow GD. In making this choice, Tobias chooses to trade one dream for the other. He clings to a desire to remain relevant; a desire for an identity which still utilizes the skills he learned as a Divergent member of the Dauntless faction. Therefore, he avoids the need for a significant re-evaluation of everything he was taught to value by immersing himself in the dream world of being GD.

Nita and her companions call for the destruction of the evil demon—the Bureau. In order to ensure Tobias's continued belief in the righteousness of their cause, Nita withholds crucial information about her plan from him. Because Tobias doesn't have enough knowledge, he behaves in a way which directly results in the death of Uriah. By withholding information which would allow Tobias to make an informed choice, and deceiving him into compliance, Nita becomes the evil demon herself.

When Descartes examines his personal beliefs and assumptions, he notes that we should refrain from acting, if we don't have all of the relevant information. If we choose to act without understanding all of the facts, we aren't just being deceived—we're actually deceiving ourselves. When we choose to remain ignorant, we must also accept the blame if this self-deception has negative consequences. Likewise, Tobias must accept the consequences of believing Nita and her followers without question:

I wanted to believe they were all wrong about me, that I am not limited by my genes, that I am no more damaged than any other person.
But how can that be true, when my actions landed Uriah in the hospital, when Tris can't even look me in the eye, when so many people
died? (*Allegiant*, p. 304)

There's always a danger in blindly following the doctrines of
strangers, but Tobias's self-deception is made doubly worse
because he's already learned the lesson that he shouldn't trust
information he is given without attempting to judge the truth of
it. Wasn't he deceived by his own mother in *Insurgent*? Didn't he
just awaken from the Cartesian dream constructed by the
Bureau controlling the Chicago experiment? The fact that he so
willingly submits to Nita's deception, despite Tris's adamant
arguments that he stop and reflect on the information given to
him, indicates his continued submission to the Cartesian dream.

Waking from the Dream

So how should we react to the evil demon's lies? How do we
respond when we awaken from our dreams to discover a world
so much bigger and more complex than we'd imagined?
Descartes would have us constantly seeking and questioning
new knowledge, because by learning more about the world, we
learn more about ourselves and our place within it. Through
that self-examination we can make an informed choice about
what we actually value and believe.

Peter's reaction to the loss of the faction system is subdued
compared to the rest of the characters. During the series, Peter
is frequently shown in the background assessing the situation—waiting and reflecting before choosing how to act. Peter's
behavior is portrayed negatively because it reflects his ability
to switch sides when he feels that it will benefit him. There is,
however, an advantage to this behavior. When Peter assesses a
situation, he decides whether he's still in a position to benefit,
or whether he must take action to ensure his continued safety
and comfort. Most readers will agree that Peter's behavior isn't
exactly admirable as a moral standard, but Descartes was concerned with the nature of reality and knowledge, not morality.

During *Allegiant*, when the characters learn that their faction system is a constructed experiment, Peter reacts with his

customary shrewd calculation. By the end of *Insurgent*, Peter has begun to question whether his ability to emotionally detach and cause pain for pleasure is desirable, as demonstrated when he occasionally shows empathy to Tris: "Peter leans forward and looks into my eyes. 'The serum will go into effect in one minute', he says. 'Be brave, Tris.'" He takes his awakening from the Cartesian dream as an opportunity to rationalize his behavior during *Divergent* and *Insurgent*. He begins pouring over maps, making notes about the planet's size and the amount of people in it. He points out to Tobias that the size of Chicago is negligible when compared to the rest of the world, and this ought to be enough to render all of his behaviors moot. Tobias, naturally, replies that these rationalizing behaviors are not enough to absolve Peter of the guilt he ought to be feeling:

> He shakes his head again, and I wonder, suddenly, if this is how he comforts himself: by convincing himself that the bad things he's done don't matter. I see how the mammoth planet that terrifies me seems like a haven to him, a place where he can disappear into its great space, never distinguishing himself, and never being held responsible for his actions. (*Allegiant*, p. 330)

For Peter, gathering information is a way for him to identify a place for himself in the world. When he realizes that Tobias is right, and that the knowledge of his own insignificance in the world isn't enough to absolve his guilt, he chooses to drink memory serum and start learning new behaviors from scratch: "I want the serum because I'm sick of being this way . . . I'm sick of doing bad things and liking it and then wondering what's wrong with me. I want it to be over. I want to start again."

Drinking the memory serum and obliterating his own personality is recognition of Descartes's final conclusion: that the only thing Descartes can be absolutely sure of is his own mind. Peter is absolutely sure of his own mind, and the behaviors and decision-making practices that have been engrained within it, and that's enough to make him want to start afresh: awakening from the Cartesian dream by erasing the deceptions of the faction system which taught him to be ruthless and cruel, re-learning everything that he has been taught to value.

Usually Only My Dreams Make This Little Sense

Tris Prior is a *curious* character. As Tori says, after Tris's faction test in *Divergent*, "Never met a curious Abnegation before." It's one of the first traits other characters recognize in her, and it surprises them. Tris's curiosity gets her into trouble more often than not, but the way she approaches the acquisition of knowledge is particularly praiseworthy from a Cartesian perspective because her desire for knowledge results in a constant re-evaluation of who she is and what she believes in. While she begins the series as a rash, dangerously impulsive character, she grows to become more reserved in her approach to new evidence; examining each new fact for falsehoods before acting, and trusting her instincts as to what is real or not. Like Descartes, she learns to trust what she knows to be true—her own mind.

Tris cannot understand why the factionless are not grateful to learn that there's a world outside of the walls of their reality. For her, the acquisition of knowledge is always positive. Tris engages with information as an almost tangible entity. She nurtures it, protects it from those who would destroy it, and shares it with as many other people as possible. Her exile from Amity headquarters is a result of her violent opposition to Peter, who attempts to steal a hard drive with the records of the Erudite using Dauntless to kill the Abnegation. Tris's personal happiness and sense of safety relies on having all of the information available to her, and when information is withheld, she feels dangerously vulnerable because she cannot act with any agency—she can only react to the decisions of other characters. She's constantly questioning whether she can trust other characters' intentions because she doesn't know them the way that she knows herself. Caleb's betrayal is a particularly hard blow to her world view because it shatters the assumptions she had made about her family and the love that they shared. Likewise, one of the biggest problems facing Tris's relationship with Tobias is that neither of them feels compelled to communicate with the other, and their secrets make it difficult to know where they stand at any given time.

Tris also finds the blind faith other experiment escapees have in the Bureau to be almost laughable, particularly when they are all aware of the continuing deceits preventing the subjects of the Chicago experiment from awakening from their dream:

> That strikes me as naive, for someone who once lived in my city and saw, at least on the screens, how many secrets we kept from one another. Evelyn tried to control people by controlling weapons, but Jeanine was more ambitious—she knew that when you control information, or manipulate it, you don't need force to keep people under your thumb. They stay there willingly. That is what the Bureau—and the entire government, probably—is doing: conditioning people to be happy under its thumb. (*Allegiant*, pp. 345–346)

At this point in the narrative, Tris has learned the hard way not to take information presented at face value. You never know where the evil demon may be lurking!

Your Life's a Lie, Now What?

What's the point of having values, if there's always a chance that those values will be proven false? In short, values define us. Through them, we construct our own understanding of who we are and our place in our world. It may be easier to allow those values to remain unchallenged, but then we risk deceiving ourselves by acting with limited information. In that case, we don't even need a demon to trick us or make us believe in false information—we do a perfectly good job of it ourselves.

When Descartes supposes that an evil demon has control over his mind and thoughts, he responds by testing what he believes to be true. This may require some personal reflection, particularly with regards to the values and ideals which make up his personal identity, but he believes that it's necessary to test himself to ensure that what he believes is still true. By confronting the demon and its lies, Descartes awakens himself from the dream. He comes away with a better understanding of the world—the *real* world—and his place in it.

When Tris wakes completely from the dream, she makes decisions and acts on behalf of all other dreamers who remain under the deceptive control of the evil demons in the Bureau. This is where the philosophy of Descartes is put to practical use. By choosing to liberate the subjects of the Chicago experiment, Tris chooses to obliterate the power the Bureau uses to control them. As Joanna Reyes and her fellow Allegiant make clear, the value placed in the faction system is strong enough for people to resist any changes to it. Instead of engaging every individual in the philosophical debate necessary to awaken them, Tris removes the deceit entirely.

The subjects of the Chicago experiment, thus awakened, are allowed the opportunity to continue identifying themselves through the faction system without the threat of control. They have awoken from their Cartesian dream, and now they can make informed choices about what they value.

18
The Virtues of Choosing Your Faction

JORDAN PASCOE

"I stare into my own eyes for a moment. Today is the day of the aptitude test that will show me which of the five factions I belong in." The aptitude test is a key institution in the world of *Divergent*. All sixteen-year-olds take the test—a simulation of a series of choices—and their responses help to determine which of the five factions they should select at the Choosing Ceremony.

The test begins with a choice: do you take a hunk of cheese or a knife? The choice determines how you'll react when a dog attacks you in the simulation: will you fight, thus ruling out Amity, or offer the dog some cheese, thus ruling out Dauntless? Each choice rules out one faction, helping you to narrow down which faction you have an aptitude for by a process of elimination.

The premise of the test is that everyone is ideally suited to one, and only one, of the factions. In many cases, people seem to have an aptitude for the faction they were raised in, so that their experience, the values they've been taught, and their aptitude all line up. If their capacities fit a different faction, however, they become transfers, leaving behind their family, faction, and the values on which they were raised. But the faction test is meant to be *informative*—as Tris reminds Caleb, "the tests don't have to change our choices." The choice is up to each individual, and making that choice is ultimately about choosing who you *want* to be.

How Deep Are Your Virtues?

The factions in *Divergent* are organized around a particular virtue: honesty, kindness, intelligence, courage, and selflessness. Virtues are positive character traits, and the idea of virtues goes back a long, long way, at least to the ancient Greeks. For the ancient Greeks, to be virtuous was to be morally excellent. *Divergent*'s faction system might be seen as harnessing and streamlining the ancient Greek idea of virtue, creating a social system in which everyone is encouraged to develop the virtues for which they have the greatest aptitude.

For Aristotle (384–322 B.C.E.), there are two kinds of virtues: intellectual virtues, which are the virtues we can be taught, and moral virtues, which are the virtues that we practice. So, when Tris's mother responds to her questions at the dinner table by asking, "Why don't you take this opportunity to listen to your father?" she's gently teaching Tris the intellectual virtue of selflessly listening to others. When Tris practices this without thinking about it—when she later makes a habit of listening to Christina, or to Four, she's *practicing* the moral virtue of listening to others. We learn virtues from our parents, teachers, and communities—as well as from books and the culture itself. But *being* virtuous means taking the virtues we've been taught to heart, practicing them on a daily basis, and allowing them to become our deepest, most ingrained habits. When virtues become habit, Aristotle suggests, they truly become part of us: virtue is really a state of character. So, for Aristotle, if I do enough selfless things, I will eventually become a selfless person, for whom selfless acts come naturally.

For Aristotle, I become selfless in three ways. First, I need to be taught the virtue of selflessness by those around me. Second, I need to have an aptitude for selflessness. And third, I need to develop a character that is disposed towards selflessness. In the opening of *Divergent*, Tris has the first of these covered: she's surrounded by selfless people who perform selfless acts, and so, she has learned the intellectual virtue of selflessness. But that doesn't mean it comes naturally to her—"faction customs dictate even idle behavior and supersede individual preferences. I doubt all the Erudite want to study all the time, or that every Candor enjoys a lively debate, but they can't defy the norms of their factions any more than I can," reflects Tris in the moments before her test. This sort of thinking reveals her own deep resistance to the norms, or virtues, of Abnegation.

Aristotle argues that our virtues are intimately connected to our functions: we choose a series of roles in life, and these roles will determine what sorts of virtues we need to develop. So, if I choose to be a doctor, I need to develop the virtues of practicing medicine, like caring, listening, and researching. If I choose to be a pianist I need to develop the virtues of a musician, which include discipline and practice. The factions in *Divergent* operate in much the same way: choosing a faction means choosing your function in life, and in doing so, it means committing to a specific set of virtues to strive for in every part of your life.

Aristotle thinks that if we choose our function well, we'll find ourselves in a state of flourishing: when our deepest desires line up with our obligations, then it's easy to fulfill those obligations and thus, to be virtuous. *Flourishing*, in a sense, means being exactly what and where you are supposed to be. So Tris's friend Susan, for example, was raised in Abnegation, and at her Choosing Ceremony, she chooses Abnegation. This is clearly her aptitude, her choice, and—lucky for her—the faction she grew up in. For Susan, the faction system works. All her values align, and she gets to be virtuous in the way that's most natural to her, the way she's been taught, and the way she's chosen. Susan, in other words, flourishes in the faction system.

Not everyone is so lucky. For some people, the aptitude test reveals an aptitude for a faction other than their own, and this forces them to make a tough choice—a choice between their upbringing (intellectual virtue) and their aptitude (state of character). This is a difficult choice, both because it means abandoning one's family and community and therefore the values with which one has been raised, and because it means choosing to learn a whole new set of values that are part of belonging to a new community. This process, clearly, can be a barrier to flourishing. For Al, choosing Dauntless means leaving his family and embarking on a whole new life, and this causes him great pain and inner conflict. Al doesn't flourish under the faction system, precisely because it pits his aptitude for virtue against the intellectual virtue of the community in which he was raised.

A Flourishing Divergent

For Susan and Al, the aptitude test gave a clear-cut answer: it ruled out four factions, and gave each of them a definitive answer about where their aptitude for virtue lies. For Tris, the choice isn't as simple. That's because Tris's aptitude test shows that she's Divergent—she has an aptitude for more than one faction, or virtue. Or, to put it differently, Tris doesn't seem to have a clearly defined function: she isn't only selfless, only smart, only brave—she's all three. But, in a system dominated by factions, she can't choose to be all three—she can only choose to be one. So, like Al and Christina and the other faction transfers, she's got a tough choice to make: her character doesn't match up with her upbringing, and so, she finds herself forced to make a choice that may undermine her flourishing and alienate her from the people she loves.

Tris's choice, however, is more complicated than Al's or Christina's, because it isn't simply a choice between her aptitude and her upbringing. Tris doesn't have a single natural aptitude or virtue, and so she has to choose which of her aptitudes to develop. If she chooses Erudite, she'll be supported in the development of her intelligence and curiosity, and if she chooses Dauntless, she'll be given the tools she needs to develop her natural aptitude for bravery. Within the world of *Divergent*, Tris doesn't have a single natural aptitude, so Aristotle's story about virtue as a state of character might not offer Tris the kind of guidance she needs in order to flourish. Without a single natural aptitude, Tris's choice is of a different nature than those of the other sixteen-year-olds who take the test. Tris has to choose between multiple virtues: does she think it is most valuable to be brave, smart, or selfless? She has an aptitude for all three, but she alone gets to choose which to dedicate herself to.

The Dangers of Virtue

In this sense, Tris's choice of faction looks less like Aristotle's theory of virtue, and more like the theory of virtue developed—nearly two thousand years later—by Immanuel Kant (1724–1804). Kant suggests we have natural aptitudes for virtues, just like Aristotle does, but he argues that what matters is not what your natural aptitudes are, but what you do with them. So the question isn't how smart or brave you are, but what actions you choose to undertake with your intelligence or courage. Kant differentiates between the virtues as *gifts of nature* and *good will*. Gifts of nature are our natural aptitudes, while good will guides us to use our virtues in the right ways and for the right reasons.

Kant points out that having natural virtues, or aptitudes, isn't enough to make you good. I could be super-intelligent, for example, but I could choose to use that intelligence in order to drug and control others—say, by developing a mind-control serum that turns otherwise good people into mindless killing machines who'll even turn on their own families. The virtues themselves can just as easily become vices if they're used in the wrong sorts of ways—as the Erudite faction so nicely demonstrates by the end of *Divergent*. So, it isn't the intelligence itself that's good, it's what I choose to do with it. For Kant, when we act in morally good ways for the right sorts of reasons, then our actions are virtuous.

So, Kant would tell Tris that her range of natural aptitudes is wonderful—it's a gift. But she also has a responsibility to use her gifts properly—the greater our gifts, the greater our responsibility to use them in the right sorts of ways. For Tris, then, what's the faction that'll best allow her to properly use her gifts?

Variety of Duties

Generally speaking, we might say that Tris has a duty to her family, who are Abnegation. Her family raised her, taught her, and cared for her; and she knows that to leave them is a betrayal of her upbringing. When her brother Caleb chooses Erudite at the Choosing Ceremony, her first thought is of her duty to her family: "I set my jaw. I will be the child that stays. I have to do this for my family. I have to."

For Aristotle, who argues that our sense of virtue is shaped by our upbringing, and by the intellectual virtues we've been raised with, this might be enough to decide it: Tris has both a duty to Abnegation, and an aptitude for Abnegation, and this seems to suggest that her duty lies in choosing the faction of her family.

Kant complicates this story of duty by distinguishing between perfect duties we *must* fulfill, and imperfect duties that we *should* fulfill. We must fulfill our perfect duties, since failing to do so would be morally wrong. Kant thinks we have two sorts of duties to ourselves. We have a perfect duty to preserve ourselves: committing suicide, on Kant's account, is morally wrong; and we have more general perfect duties to not take any course of action that would undermine our capacity for morality. So, on these grounds, he warns us that we have duties not to destroy ourselves with drink and drugs, and not to let ourselves be destroyed by strong desires for sex or violence.

Kant also says we have imperfect duties: duties that are good to fulfill, but it would not be immoral for us to choose not to fulfill them. For instance, when Susan's father offers Tris and Caleb a ride home, he's doing something good out of a sense of duty, but it wouldn't be wrong for him *not* to offer them a ride. Likewise, Kant would say that Tris's obligation to her family is an imperfect duty: it would undoubtedly be good for her to be "the one that stays," but that doesn't mean that it's wrong for her to leave.

Kant maintains that, as moral beings, we have imperfect duties to try to develop ourselves. For example, he says in *Groundwork of the Metaphysics of Morals*, that if you have a particular skill or talent for something, you have an imperfect duty to develop that talent. These duties, he thinks, have everything to do with having respect for yourself as an inherently valuable being—so out of respect for yourself, you should try to make yourself the best version of yourself that you can be.

With that said, for Kant, we have duties to ourselves and to others. But the duties to ourselves must come before our duties to others, since our duties to ourselves concern developing our capacity to be good, rational, moral people—and thus to have the capacity to fulfill our duties to others. But this doesn't necessarily mean Tris can abandon her imperfect duties to her family and faction. Kant might argue that Tris's duty to her family and to Abnegation is really a duty *to* herself *regarding* her family and faction: Tris has an imperfect duty to herself to cultivate the qualities of being a loving daughter, for example, and this means that she has a duty to herself to stand by her family and faction. When she says "I will be the child that stays," she's reminding herself of a duty to herself—a duty to be a certain kind of person.

Kant would, also, likely agree with Caleb's decision to fulfill his imperfect duty to himself by developing his natural capacity for intellectual curiosity over his imperfect duty to his family and faction. Kant would certainly admit that Caleb has duties regarding Abnegation, and his family, for raising, teaching, and nurturing him, but he can't ignore the duties to himself. He has an aptitude for intelligence, and so, out of respect for himself, he has a duty to try to develop that aptitude. Of course, he has a perfect duty to develop his aptitudes in a morally good way—his intelligence is only good when it's combined with a good will. But as long as he chooses to develop his intelligence in the right ways for the right reasons, Kant would say that he's made the right choice.

For Tris, however, things are more complicated. She can't choose to develop all of her natural capacities, because the faction system forces her to choose only one. The faction system limits her capacity to be, as Four puts it, "smart *and* selfless *and* caring *and* honest *and* brave." She must choose. And certainly, she has duties to others—to Abnegation, the people who raised and taught her—but she has obligations to herself, too. So, what should Tris do?

Kant would say that any choice that doesn't violate a perfect duty is a good choice, and as long as she chooses for the right sort of reasons, there appear to be no perfect duties violated by any of her options. Therefore, she would be right to choose Abnegation, if she felt that the most compelling reason was her imperfect duty regarding her parents, friends, and the people who raised her. If she chooses Abnegation for fear of facing the unknown, then her choice isn't based on good reason, but fear, and so it would be a bad decision. As long as she acts out of a sense of duty, and out of respect for herself for knowing and choosing her duty, her choice is a good, moral choice.

She would also be right to choose Dauntless, if she chose it out of a sense of duty to herself. Tris feels drawn to the Dauntless, and to a part of herself that identifies with the virtues of Dauntless. It's a part of herself she's at once afraid of and compelled by, and so, there's a sense in which Tris has an imperfect duty to herself to develop her capacity for bravery. This choice will drive her to face her fears and develop her natural capacities for bravery—although, she's unaware that along the way it'll also put her in positions where she acts contrary to duty, by hurting herself and others. If it were reasonable for her to know this, it might change the nature of her decision, but with such knowledge, it's a good choice.

Despite his emphasis on the importance of intellectual virtues, Aristotle, too, might agree with Tris's choice to become Dauntless. Aristotle thought that bravery was the greatest and noblest of the virtues, since it involves a willingness to give our lives for something greater than ourselves. The key distinction to see is that for Aristotle, Tris's choice has to do with the *nature of the virtues* involved, rather than with the *nature of Tris's choice*, which is what Kant emphasizes.

Choosing for Ourselves

Because Tris has a true choice about what faction to choose, she's also fully responsible for the nature of that choice. This means that when she discovers that the Dauntless are being controlled by the Erudite, and that she's in the position of doing morally questionable things, she has a duty to make new choices. After all, being dauntless isn't in itself a virtue—as Kant reminds us, bravery is good, but only if it's combined with a good will. For example, Eric's leadership of the Dauntless, under Jeanine's influence, isn't guided by a good will, but by a desire for power, and a willingness to use anyone to get it. Eric's bravery and intelligence aren't morally good, from a Kantian perspective, because they're being used in morally evil ways. And this means that, in a certain sense, they are no longer virtues.

The choices that Tris faces after she joins Dauntless make a strong case for choosing a Kantian conception of virtue over an Aristotelian one. After all, Aristotle argues that our virtues are determined by our natural capacities and by the values we've been taught. Hence, being Dauntless would mean developing an aptitude for bravery in the ways prescribed by those who lead and shape the Dauntless faction, and we've already seen what sorts of evils can result from this approach.

Because Aristotelian virtue places such a strong emphasis on flourishing, and therefore, on living in ways that are harmonious with the values of our community, it can be difficult to resist our community when their virtues are corrupted. For most of the Dauntless initiates, the only way to survive is to adopt the definition of bravery that Eric and other Dauntless subscribe to: bravery means steeling oneself to overcome fear and to silence the doubts inside us. And, as it turns out, this definition of courage is quite useful in creating an army that follows orders without question. The definition of virtue that the majority of Dauntless subscribe to, in other words, is a corrupted ideal. Sadly, being part of the Dauntless community in Roth's narrative requires initiates and members alike to take this shared definition as an ideal, and to build their characters in accordance with it.

Kant, on the other hand, introduces a moral compass outside of virtue: our virtues are virtuous only if they are guided by the good will. For instance, Tobias has a different understanding of bravery. He thinks that bravery and selflessness aren't all that different, and he reminds Tris that she's her most courageous when she's also her most selfless—like when she volunteers to take Al's place in the shooting range. Tobias's understanding of the virtues of dauntlessness is guided by a deeper sense of responsibility, and this allows him to resist the dominant definition and to think for himself. Kant would be proud!

Because Tris is Divergent, she's already had to think for herself, outside of the logic of the faction system. When Tobias points out that she's most brave when she is selfless, she wonders, "Am I wired like the Abnegation, or the Dauntless?" The answer that comes to her highlights her ability to think for herself: "maybe the answer is neither. Maybe I am wired like the Divergent."

With this ability to think for herself outside of the logic of the faction system, comes a responsibility to make her choices carefully, based on her duties to herself and others. So, once Tris knows Eric's true motives, she knows that he's twisted the Dauntless into something that is no longer virtuous. This gives her an obligation to resist this corrupt definition of dauntlessness, and weigh it against other morally sound obligations. This choice is available to her in part because she's learned to think for herself about what counts as a true virtue, like a Kantian, rather than merely choosing between the virtues others have offered her.

19

Why Divergent Are Actually Convergent

KYLE A. SCHENKEWITZ

In *Divergent*, the city of Chicago is a world unto itself, literally. Fenced in, separated from the outside by myth, history, and ignorance, the inhabitants of Chicago have a reality defined by their pursuit of peace. Their society is structured around the idea that a division of labor and a division of virtue are the means of preserving peace and avoiding warfare.

As the story unfolds, the defects of this constructed reality become more and more apparent. But, we wonder, why does this society fail when its goals are so admirable? The society is intent on forming individuals according to particular virtues, and it reinforces the pursuit of virtue through ritual and lifestyle, down to the smallest detail. It recognizes individual potential for greatness according to society's values. Yet, things go awry and the city's pursuit of a peaceful and humane way of life is thwarted.

Chicago built their society around the idea of promoting individual virtues, but the problem is they overlooked the need to cultivate multiple virtues at the same time. Cultivating multiple virtues is the only way to achieve the peace they desire. Ironically, individuals labeled "Divergent," who represent the goal of each individual in society, are labeled as pariahs. For Roth, the central character Tris (Beatrice) displays an aptitude for numerous factions and, as such, is labeled "Divergent." Yet, her status as Divergent isn't a deficiency in the narrative but a fullness of human character. Tris is the novel's protagonist because she eschews the social norm of adhering to a single virtue, and uses all of her virtues to help choose the right path.

As Roth's account shows, particular virtues must *converge* within each person for justice to flourish. Tris, like the other Divergent, embodies not just one singular virtue, but the convergence of all the virtues in a unity of character. In the end, Divergent aren't the source of society's ills, but the locus for a more fully-human and peaceful existence to be realized.

The Worldview of Divergent

At the age of sixteen, each member of Chicago must choose a faction into which they will spend the rest of their lives. The rationale for dividing society into five factions is carefully explained each year at the Choosing Ceremony. When Tris must make her choice, Marcus Eaton explains why their society has developed this ceremony and rigid system of division. He recounts, "It has been this way since the beginning of the great peace, when the factions were formed. I think the system persists because we're afraid of what might happen if it didn't: war." Their world had been rocked by warfare and other evils due to the conflicts of human personalities, "humankind's inclination toward evil, in whatever form that is." The people of Chicago divided into factions to eradicate society's ills. As Marcus explains, "Those who blamed aggression formed Amity . . . Those who blamed ignorance became the Erudite . . . Those who blamed duplicity created Candor . . . Those who blamed selfishness made Abnegation . . . And those who blamed cowardice were the Dauntless . . ."

The peace Chicago had enjoyed since the division was due to the contributions of each faction to the whole of society:

> Abnegation has fulfilled our need for selfless leaders in government; Candor has provided us with trustworthy and sound leaders in law; Erudite has supplied us with intelligent teachers and researchers; Amity has given us understanding as counselors and caretakers; Dauntless provides us with protection from threats both within and without.

Each faction has their role to play in society, and each role is uniquely suited to the type of virtue the faction champions. Not only were the factions conducive to a peaceful society, but as Tris reminds Four in *Allegiant*, "A long time ago, a group of people decided that the faction system would be the best way to live—or the way to get people to life the best lives they could."

Choosing a faction was also for your personal good. Cultivating courage, honesty, selflessness, understanding, or intellect is how you achieved the good for yourself. Each resident of Chicago must choose a faction, must choose a way to live in this society. Factions give the people of Chicago meaning, purpose, and life: "Without a faction, we have no purpose and no reason to live." As the story opens, Beatrice explains, "Today is the day of the aptitude test that will show me which of the five factions I belong in. And tomorrow, at the Choosing Ceremony, I will decide on a faction; I will decide the rest of my life; I will decide to stay with my family or abandon them."

Familial ties that bind child to parent are broken when a child chooses a faction different from the one in which they were reared. This hard choice between family and faction is guided by a quote in each child's Faction History textbook: "Faction before blood." Beatrice knows that "more than family, our factions are where we belong." Choosing a different faction is choosing a new identity, a new name, a new way of living in the world.

Beatrice of Abnegation

Each faction focuses on a single virtue as central to its communal identity. This virtue is instilled through habitual actions. The factions believe that you acquire virtue by practicing virtue, you become what you do. As the narrative moves from Beatrice's experiences as Abnegation to her life as Dauntless, the central virtue of each is communally and personally embodied through rituals that make and re-make a person. She fully understands at this moment that the person she was with her family in Abnegation will be altered at a very fundamental level, to affect her dress, her actions, and even her thinking.

As a child in an Abnegation family, classmates derided her as a "stiff." This moniker is appropriate because of the way Abnegation live their lives of selflessness. Their neighborhoods are austere and plain:

> The houses on my street are all the same size and shape. They are made of grey cement, with few windows, in economical, no-nonsense

rectangles. Their lawns are crabgrass and their mailboxes are dull metal. To some the sight might be gloomy, but to me their simplicity is comforting.

Abnegations lived in simplicity and avoided any attention to the self: "The grey clothes, the plain hairstyle, and the unassuming demeanor of my faction are supposed to make it easier for me to forget myself, and easier for everyone else to forget me too."

Every aspect of their life is directed to instilling and supporting the virtue of selflessness. They walk, talk, and eat in a manner that is distinctively Abnegation and decidedly self-diminishing:

> The reason for the simplicity isn't disdain for uniqueness, as the other factions have sometimes interpreted it. Everything—our houses, our clothes, our hairstyles—is meant to help us forget ourselves and to protect us from vanity, greed, and envy, which are just forms of self-ishness. If we have little, and want for little, and we are all equal, we envy no one. I try to love it.

The stark existence of Abnegation provides a comfort, but for some, like Beatrice, it engenders a desire for more.

This scenario of virtue, instilled through an intentional way of life, is the means to teach the signature virtue of each faction. Learning through habituated action is a way of embodying a virtue. Children in each faction are reared in their particular lifestyle. Beatrice recalls the regularity of her haircuts and the distinctive activity of viewing herself in a mirror only on those occasions: "There is one mirror in my house. It is behind a sliding panel in the hallway upstairs. Our faction allows me to stand in front of it on the second day of every third month, the day my mother cuts my hair." She's only reminded of her physical self four times each year, every other day she's trained to forget.

She can imagine the impact of Candor-rearing as she encounters a Candor man who "wears a black suit with a white tie—Candor standard uniform. Their faction values honesty and sees the truth as black and white, so that is what they wear." Each day, the Candors would dress, presumably in front of a mirror, and be reminded of the stark distinction between truth and falsity. Abnegation always hovered in the in-between, wearing only shades of grey.

Tris of Dauntless

The transformation from Beatrice of Abnegation to Tris of Dauntless is a remarkable shift. Beatrice's first recognition of this change occurred moments after choosing Dauntless in the Choosing Ceremony. Following her new faction she recalls:

> I have not run anywhere in a long time. Abnegation discourages anything done strictly for my own enjoyment, and that is what this is: my lungs burning, my muscles aching, the fierce pleasure of a flat-out sprint. I follow the Dauntless down the street and around the corner and hear a familiar sound: the train horn.

Her recognition is complete when a girl falls to her death due to the crippling fear of jumping from a moving train. Beatrice must confront her new reality. This one girl's death was as much a part of Dauntless life as a Candor's outspokenness. Beatrice bolsters herself, "as sternly as possible, *that is how we work here*. We do dangerous things and people die. People die, and we move on to the next dangerous thing. The sooner that lesson sinks in, the better chance I have at surviving initiation." Her new faction confronts situations in a manner wholly distinct from the way she was reared.

Life as Dauntless is more than just a change in name, but the construction of a whole new identity, a wholly new way of seeing and being in the world. When Beatrice takes her first leap as a new Dauntless she is invited to take a new name, Tris. She considers her transformation from Abnegation to Dauntless internally, pondering, "A new place, a new name. I can be remade here." For Tris, this new reality is symbolized in some very basic activities. Her move to the Dauntless dormitory involves co-habitation with males. She copes with this strange arrangement by clinging to a vestige of her old life, her Abnegation clothing:

> I have never slept in the same room as a boy before, but here I have no other option, unless I want to sleep in the hallway. Everyone else changed into the clothes the Dauntless provided for us, but I sleep in

my Abnegation clothes, which still smell like soap and fresh air, like home.

The shift to Dauntless life weighs heavily on Tris, as new values are thrust upon her. Shedding her Abnegation clothing and donning new Dauntless clothes becomes a pivotal moment for Tris, not only because of the clothing itself, but also because she must now face her new self in an Abnegation-prohibited activity. Tris looks at herself in the mirror, "for the first time I stare openly at my own reflection. My heart rate picks up as I do, like I am breaking the rules and will be scolded for it. It will be difficult to break the habits of thinking Abnegation instilled in me, like tugging a single thread from a complex work of embroidery. But I will find new habits, new thoughts, new rules. I will become something else."

All of the other new Dauntless initiates undergo similar transformations. In a poignant passage, the ex-Candor, Peter, must halter his tongue when a loaded gun is placed to his head by a Dauntless member, Four (Tobias): Four lowers the gun. "Once the immediate threat is gone, Peter's green eyes harden. I'm surprised he can stop himself from responding, after speaking his mind all his life in Candor, but he does, his cheeks red." The Candor habit of outspokenness is hindered only through threat of death, as Peter, too, is learning a new way of being in the Dauntless world.

Yet, the deeply embodied habits of her life as Abnegation are never truly excised. When Tris's mother visits her at Dauntless, Tris reverts back to her Abnegation way of life where children always defer to their parents in conversation, often speaking only when addressed. Her mother gently asks, "Tell me how you are." Tris simply responds, "You first." Tris understands that in this interaction with her mother after weeks in the Dauntless lair, "The old habits are back. I should let her speak first. I shouldn't let the conversation stay focused on myself for too long. I should make sure she doesn't need anything." Again, amid the chaos of Chicago's social disintegration, Tris solemnly reflects:

The dormitory, at least, is quiet. I stare at my plate of food. I just grabbed what looked good to me at the time, and now I take a closer look, I realize that I chose a plain chicken breast, a scoop of peas, and a piece of brown bread. Abnegation food. I sigh. Abnegation is what I am. It is what I am when I'm not thinking about what I'm doing. It is what I am when I am put to the test. It is what I am even when I appear to be brave. Am I in the wrong faction?

Try as she may, Tris can never fully abandon the habits and way of life instilled in her Abnegation childhood.

Virtue Beyond Faction

The people of Chicago envisioned peaceful existence through cultivating a single virtue as a faction community. Yet, even amid the momentary peace, the factions view one another as flawed and incomplete. Tris's father decries the Dauntless as "'hellions.' They are pierced, tattooed, and black-clothed. Their primary purpose is to guard the fence that surrounds our city." The interdependency of the factions is combined with tension. Each faction depends upon the others, but they often view the other factions as deficient in some way. In *Insurgent*, Candor is depicted as honest but insensitive: "The Candor sing the praises of truth, but they never tell you how much it costs." Candor are able to recognize the faults in Dauntless and Erudite, singing:

> Dauntless is the cruelest of the five
> They tear each other to pieces . . .
> Erudite is the coldest of the five
> Knowledge is a costly thing . . .

Throughout the series, Roth asserts the insufficiency of solitary virtues. Chicago's peace is compromised when certain factions overstep the boundaries of their faction. The antagonism that leads to Chicago's chaos stems from concentration on a single virtue, which actually transforms their virtue into a vice. A key example of this is that because Erudite don't value Amity and Abnegation, their pursuit for knowledge is transformed into a pursuit of power and dominance. Tris's father discusses this tendency early in *Divergent*: "Valuing knowledge above all else results in a lust for power, and that leads men into dark and empty places. We should be thankful that we know better."

In *Allegiant*, Tris begins to understand "that every faction loses something when it gains a virtue":

The Dauntless: Brave but cruel
The Erudite: Intelligent but vain
The Amity: Peaceful but passive
The Candor: honest but inconsiderate
The Abnegation: selfless but stifling

The ideals of Chicago's society deteriorate simply because the virtues of each faction aren't integrated into society as a whole, but held as distinct for each faction. The factions produce malformed individuals that fail to see how the stability of the city depends upon the interrelatedness of the factions. More tragic still is the recognition that the very structure of Chicago's peace is the means of its demise.

Tris, as Divergent, recognizes that her adoption of the Dauntless way of life will always be incomplete, she will always be partially Abnegation. In Chicago, this is viewed as a fault. She hasn't fully adopted the virtue of her chosen faction. She's neither put faction before blood, nor has she assented to the superiority of her Dauntless virtue. Tris considers:

> I wanted to be like the Dauntless I saw at school. I wanted to be loud and daring and free like them . . . No I was wrong; I didn't jump off the roof because I wanted to be like the Dauntless. I jumped off because I already was like them, and I wanted to show myself to them. I wanted to acknowledge a part of myself that Abnegation demanded I hide.

As Divergent, Tris understands that embodying the courage of Dauntless doesn't negate the selflessness of Abnegation. Nor does it contradict the wisdom of the Erudite and the goodwill of Amity. While each faction's contribution to Chicago's peace necessitates the strengthening of a particular virtue, the move to specialization in one and only one virtue leads to Chicago's downfall. Tris, like the other Divergent, understands that the good for each person and the good for Chicago involve each individual cultivating all the virtues.

Divergent as Convergent

For the Divergent, practicing all the virtues came naturally. Being forced to choose a single virtue was aberrant. Beatrice's aptitude test was inconclusive because she showed aptitude for multiple factions. As Dauntless, Tris's struggle to limit herself to a single virtue was a sign of her fully-developed sense of humanity. She couldn't be limited to a single virtue, but pursued a unity of virtue in herself. On the eve of the Choosing ceremony, Tris's brother Caleb had already chosen his faction, Erudite: "I peer into his room and see an unmade bed and a stack of books on his desk." Caleb's choice is clear: he'd already begun to distance himself from the simplicity and orderliness of Abnegation and began hoarding knowledge as an Erudite. For Beatrice, life was not so simple. She faced struggles within herself that Caleb never faced. When the factionless man grabbed her apples, Beatrice thinks, "I am ready. I know what to do. I picture myself bringing my elbow back and hitting him. I see the bag of apples flying away from me. I hear my running footsteps. I am prepared to act."

Her upbringing in Abnegation should've fully trained her to simply give her apples away. The internal conflict she displays reveals the complexity of her nature, as opposed to her brother. Caleb, Beatrice tells us, was always the ideal Abnegation child. Even though he eventually chose Erudite, he was able to seamlessly shift into his new role. Beatrice, on the other hand, is constantly in turmoil. She feels the pull of her old life within her new life. She seeks to be a great Dauntless initiate, but also exhibits a desire for knowledge and compassion. Tris must negotiate between the virtues, which is what makes her stronger and wiser than most other characters.

Her choices are complex and must be carefully negotiated because she has options from which to choose. She's more fully-human because she actually has choices to make. It's no wonder that Tobias sees something different and special in Tris. He reminds her, "If you throw yourself into danger for no reason again, you will have become nothing more than a Dauntless adrenaline junkie looking for a hit, and I'm not going to help you do it. I love Tris the Divergent, who makes decisions apart from faction loyalty, who isn't some faction archetype." Tris makes decisions from the deepest part of who she is and in recognition of the value of all the virtues. Her rearing and also her pursuit of various virtues have shaped her personal character.

In the Divergent, the multiplicity of virtues are at play. The readers learn in *Allegiant* that, "'Divergent' is the name we decided to give to those who have reached the desired level of genetic healing," says David. "We wanted to make sure that the leaders of your city valued them. We didn't expect the leader of Erudite to start hunting them down—or for the Abnegation to even tell her what they were." The Divergent aren't the outcasts of Chicago's society, but their apex. Divergent have aptitude for multiple virtues and these virtues are essential to the complexities of their fully realized humanity. In the Divergent, multiple virtues converge into a unified whole in each individual. Their choices are not dominated by a single virtue that demands a simple response: honesty, fearlessness, selflessness, peacefulness, or knowledge. It appears that the faction-loyal aren't able to make real choices from real alternatives because they have such a narrow view: hence, the derogatory term "Genetically Damaged."

The Divergent, however, are capable of negotiating the tensions that having multiple virtues bring to situations. In the struggle between the virtues they're able to more truly see the world and more fully understand their place within it. Upon learning the truth of Chicago's history and organization, Tris ponders:

> But now I'm wondering if I need it anymore, if we ever really *need* these words, 'Dauntless', 'Erudite', 'Divergent', 'Allegiant', or if we can just be friends or lovers or siblings, defined instead by the choices we make and the love and loyalty that binds us.

For Tris and the Divergents, every situation is an opportunity to choose what they will do, to choose who they will become. This is the foundation of what it means to be truly human.

Divergent Bibliographic Database

Aristotle. 1999. *Nicomachean Ethics*. Indianapolis: Hackett.
Asia Society. Accessed 2014. The Origins of Buddhism.
  http://asiasociety.org/origins-buddhism.
Begley, Sharon. 2009. *Train Your Mind, Change Your Brain: How a
  New Science Reveals Our Extraordinary Potential to Transform
  Ourselves*. New York: Ballantine.
Bentham, Jeremy. 1988 [1977]. *A Fragment on Government*.
  Cambridge: Cambridge University Press.
Bible. 2011. *New International Version Thinline Bible*. Grand
  Rapids: Zondervan.
Bloom, Allan. 2013 [1987]. *The Closing of the American Mind. How
  Higher Education Has Failed Democracy and Impoverished the
  Souls of Today's Students*. New York: Simon and Schuster.
Brainworks. Accessed 2014. What Are Brainwaves?
  <www.brainworksneurotherapy.com/what-are-brainwaves>.
Byerly, Catherine. Accessed 2014. 5 Business Lessons from the Hit
  Film *Divergent. Jacksonville Business Journal*. <http://jacksonville
  .icito.com/5-business-lessons-from-the-hit-film-divergent>.
Carter, Jimmy. 1979. State of the Union Address. Washington, DC.
Code, Lorraine. 1987. *Epistemic Responsibility*. Brown.
The Colbert Report, October 31st, 2011. Accessed 2014.
  <http://thecolbertreport.cc.com/videos>.
Collingwood, Jane. Accessed 2014. Side Effects of ADHD Medications.
  <http://psychcentral.com/lib/side-effects-of-adhd-medications/
  0003782>.
Connor, Ed. 2007. Psychology Bad: Why Neuroscience Is the
  Darkest Art in the Latest Whedonverse. In J. Davidson and
  L. Wilson, eds., *The Psychology of Joss Whedon: An
  Unauthorized Exploration of Buffy, Angel, and Firefly*.
  Dallas: Benbella.

Consumer Reports. Accessed 2014. The Pros and Cons of Treating ADHD with Drugs. http://www.consumerreports.org/cro/2013/01/the-pros-and-cons-of-treating-adhd-with-drugs/index.htm.

Corrigan, Michael. Accessed 2014. So They Say Your Child has ADHD? April Fools! <www.madinamerica.com/2014/03/say-child-adhd-april-fools-2>.

Crehan, Kate. 2002. *Gramsci, Culture, and Anthropology*. Berkeley: University of California Press.

Dacey, Austin. 2008. *The Secular Conscience: Why Belief Belongs in Public Life*. Amherst: Prometheus.

Daniels, Norman. 1988. *Am I My Parents' Keeper: An Essay on Justice between the Young and the Old*. New York: Oxford University Press.

Davidson, Richard J., and Sharon Begley. 2012. *The Emotional Life of Your Brain: How Its Unique Patterns Affect the Way You Think, Feel, and Live—and How You Can Change Them*. New York: Penguin.

Descartes, René. 1993. *Meditations on First Philosophy*. Indianapolis: Hackett.

DuBois, W.E.B. 1994 [1903]. *The Souls of Black Folk*. Mineola: Dover.

English, Jane. 1992. What Do Grown Children Owe Their Parents? In Nancy S. Jecker, ed., *Aging and Ethics: Philosophical Problems in Gerontology*. New York: Springer.

Foucault, Michel. 1977. Prison Talk: An Interview. *Radical Philosophy* 16.

———. 1980 [1972]. *Power / Knowledge: Selected Interviews and Other Writings, 1972–1977*. New York: Random House.

Frank, Thomas. 2001. *One Market Under God: Extreme Capitalism, Market Populism, and the End of Economic Democracy*. New York: Random House.

Freire, Paulo. 1993 [1970]. *Pedagogy of the Oppressed*. New York: Continuum.

Gandhi, Mohandas K. 1993. *The Essential Writings of Mahatma Gandhi*. New York: Oxford University Press.

Glaude, Eddie S., Jr. 1997. *Exodus: Religion, Race, and Nation in Early Nineteenth-Century Black America*. Chicago: University of Chicago Press.

Goleman, Daniel. 1995. *Emotional Intelligence: Why It Can Matter More that IQ*. New York: Bantam.

Grabovac, Andrea. Accessed 2014. The Neurobiology of Mindfulness. <www.mindfulness-matters.org/2008/11/01/the-neurobiology-of-mindfulness/>.

Gramsci, Antonio. 2000. *The Antonio Gramsci Reader*. New York: New York University Press.

Harbour, Vanessa. 2012. Creative Judgment and the Issues of Writing Young Adult Fiction. *Axon Journal* 1:2.

Herrnstein, Richard. J., and Charles Murray. 2010 [1994]. *The Bell Curve: Intelligence and Class Structure in American Life*. New York: Simon and Schuster.

Jacobs, Bob. 2005. The Myth of ADHD: Psychiatric Oppression of Children. In Judith Bessant, Richard Hill, and Rob Watts, eds., *Violations of Trust: How Social and Welfare Institutions Fail Children and Young People*. Aldershot: Ashgate.

Jones, Hillary A. 2011. "Them as Feel the Need to be Free": Reworking the Frontier Myth. *Southern Communication Journal* 76:3.

Kant, Immanuel. 1993 [1785]. *Grounding for the Metaphysics of Morals: with On a Supposed Right to Lie because of Philanthropic Concerns*. Indianapolis: Hackett.

Klineberg, O. 1934. Cultural Factors in Intelligence-Test Performance. *The Journal of Negro Education* 3:3.

Li, Puqun. 2012. *A Guide to Asian Philosophy*. Peterborough, Ontario: Broadview Press.

Marx, Karl. 1978. *The Marx-Engels Reader*. New York: Norton.

McCall, Leslie, and Jeff Manza. 2011. Class Differences in Social and Political Attitudes in the United States. In Robert Y. Shapiro and Lawrence Jacobs, eds., *Oxford Handbook of American Public Opinion and the Media*. Oxford: Oxford University Press.

McNamee, Stephen J. and Robert K. Miller, Jr. Accessed 2014. The Meritocracy Myth. <http://www.ncsociology.org/sociationtoday/v21/merit.htm>.

Meiklejohn, Alexander. 1955. Senate Committee on the Judiciary, Subcommittee on Constitutional Rights, Hearings. 84th Congress. 1st Session.

———. 1965. *Political Freedom: The Constitutional Powers of the People*. New York: Oxford University Press.

Montmarquet, James. 1992. Epistemic Virtue and Doxastic Responsibility. *American Philosophical Quarterly* 29:4.

Neiman, Susan. 2004. *Evil in Modern Thought: An Alternative History of Philosophy*. Princeton: Princeton University Press. Introduction available at www.susan-neiman.de/docs/b_preface.html.

Nietzsche, Friedrich. 2009. On the Genealogy of Morals. In Friedrich Nietzsche, *Basic Writings*. New York: Random House.

Nussbaum, Martha. 2008. *Liberty of Conscience: In Defense of America's Tradition of Religious Equality*. New York: Basic Books.

Obama, Barack. 2014. State of the Union Address. Washington, DC.

———. 2014. The White House. Tweet. 16th April, 8:32 P.M.

Perkins, John M. 2011. *Love Is the Final Fight*. Ventura: Regal.

Plato. 1997. The Republic. In *Plato: Complete Works*. Indianapolis: Hackett.

Reagan, Ronald. 1984. State of the Union Address. Washington, DC.

Rieder, Jonathan. 2013. *Gospel of Freedom: Martin Luther King, Jr.'s Letter from Birmingham Jail and the Struggle that Changed a Nation*. New York: Bloomsbury.

Roth, Veronica. 2011. *Divergent*. New York: HarperCollins.

———. 2012. *Insurgent*. New York: HarperCollins.

———. 2013. *Allegiant*. New York: HarperCollins.

———. 2013. *The World of Divergent: The Path to Allegiant*. HarperCollins.

Rousseau, Jean-Jacques. 1755. *Discourse on the Origin of Inequality*. Selections translated by Trip McCrossin.

———. 1755. *Discourse on Political Economy*. Selections translated by Trip McCrossin.

———. 1762. *The Social Contract*. Selections translated by Trip McCrossin.

———. 1762. *Émile: Or, On Education*. Selections translated by Trip McCrossin.

Sitrin, Marina, and Dario Azzellini. 2014. *They Can't Represent Us! Reinventing Democracy from Greece to Occupy*. London: Verso.

Solomon, Robert C. 1995. *A Passion for Justice: Emotions and the Origin of the Social Contract*. Lanham: Rowman and Littlefield.

Sowell, Thomas. 2013. *Intellectuals and Race*. New York: Basic Books.

Tolle, Eckhart. 2008. *The New Earth: Awakening to Your Life's Purpose*. New York: Penguin.

US National Library of Medicine. Accessed 2014. ADHD Drugs Linked to Later Weight Gain in Kids. <www.nlm.nih.gov/medlineplus/news/fullstory_145144.html>.

US News and World Report. Accessed 2014. One in 10 U.S. Kids Diagnosed with ADHD: Report. http://health.usnews.com/healthnews/news/articles/2013/04/01/one-in-10-us-kids-diagnosed-with-adhd-report.

Voltaire (François-Marie Arouet). 1759. *Candide, or Optimism*. Translated by Tobias Smollett <oll.libertyfund.org/titles/voltaire-the-works-of-voltaise-vol-i-candid>.

Washington, Booker T. 2000. *Up from Slavery*. New York: Signet.

Wolterstorff, Nicholas. 1983. *Until Justice and Peace Embrace*. Grand Rapids: Eerdmans.

———. 2008. *Justice: Rights and Wrongs*. Princeton: Princeton University Press.

———. 2011. *Justice in Love*. Grand Rapids: Eerdmans.

Zagzebski, Linda. 1996. *Virtues of the Mind: An Inquiry into the Nature of Virtue and the Ethical Foundations of Knowledge*. Cambridge: Cambridge University Press.

The Bureau of Philosophical Welfare

GREGORY L. BOCK, PhD, is Senior Lecturer in Philosophy and Religion at the University of Texas at Tyler. His research areas include ethics and the philosophy of religion, and he has co-authored several pop culture and philosophy chapters with his brother Jeff, including chapters in *Psych and Philosophy: Some Dark Juju-Magumbo* and *The Devil and Philosophy: The Nature of His Game*. He would choose to join Dauntless, but he gets sick on trains.

JEFFREY L. BOCK has an MA in History and helps manage a small web design firm in East Texas. With his unquenchable quest for knowledge, he would have picked Erudite as his faction. However, according to most rumors and reports, when faced with cutting his own hand with a knife, he ran out of the room screaming and now roams with the factionless.

CHAD A. BOGOSIAN is an Assistant Professor of Philosophy at Clovis Community College in Fresno. His philosophical interests lie at the intersection of ethics, epistemology, philosophy of the human person, and philosophy of religion. He has published articles on free will and the epistemology of disagreement. He has served on the Bioethics Committee at Phoenix Children's Hospital and is the Ethics Chair for the American Academy of Religion, Western Region. At the outset of *Divergent* (the movie), he was torn between joining Erudite and Amity, for both knowledge and service hold promise for bringing about peace in society. By the end, he most identified with Divergent, due to their having a little bit of all of the faction virtues, and empathized with their struggle to "fit" one prescribed mold.

COLE BOWMAN is a writer and independent scholar living in Portland, Oregon. She has several more projects caught in various stages of publication, including more from Open Court's Popular Culture and Philosophy series. Her fear landscape would undoubtedly be populated by each and every one of the factions' initiation rituals, so she would likely end up factionless. She is also shockingly comfortable with that outcome.

JILLIAN L. CANODE was born into Amity, but she couldn't take all the ukulele music. So she hatched a plan to create Dauntudite, a safe place where people who have tattoos and love books could hang out together. That didn't take off, so she went to graduate school, and, in 2011, she received her PhD in Philosophy and Literature from Purdue University. She likes to publish on popular culture, and she currently resides in Lima, Perú, where she teaches for The Center for Global Education at Universidad San Ignacio de Loyola.

JOHN V. KARAVITIS, CPA, MBA, a member of Erudite (*Go Owls! No Fouls!*), has dauntlessly pursued knowledge, and never abnegated his judgment that the search for practical truth must be based purely on reason. Known for fostering amity among his fellow faction members, John, a Chicago native, would like to confirm in all candor that the *Divergent* trilogy is in fact a documentary. Yes indeed.

CHRISTOPHER KETCHAM, PhD, is a peculiar: a reformed academic living in the mushroom country of Pennsylvania. Like the Divergent Tris, his capabilities are wide-ranging, from work on social justice, to philosophy and popular culture and, here's a twist, risk management, where he has contributed to and edited two books.

COURTLAND LEWIS, PhD, is Program Co-ordinator of Philosophy and Religious Studies at Owensboro Community and Technical College. He runs his own faction of rebel Philosophers, who meet in his basement to discuss how Wisdom is the only means to achieve peace. Courtland is the co-editor (with Paula Smithka) of *Doctor Who and Philosophy: Bigger On the Inside*, and of *More Doctor Who and Philosophy: Regeneration Time*. He also edited *Futurama and Philosophy*, is currently writing *Doctor Who and the Good Life*, and contributed to *Time and Relative Dimensions in Faith* and *Behind the Sofa* (a collection to aid Alzheimer's research). Wisdom before Ignorance!

GREG LITTMANN jumped from the Dauntless train. He missed the roof of the building by a foot or so, and Tris and the other initiates watched as he plummeted screaming toward the concrete below. Tris knew that he was an Associate Professor of Philosophy at Southern Illinois University Edwardsville, where he taught Epistemology, Metaphysics, and Reasoning and Argumentation. He'd told her on the train that he'd published in the philosophy of logic, evolutionary epistemology, and the philosophy of professional philosophy (no really), as well as writing many chapters for books that relate philosophy to popular culture, including volumes on *Adventure Time*, *Doctor Who*, Neil Gaiman, Roald Dahl, and *The Walking Dead*. Tris had meant to ask him why he'd chosen Dauntless instead of Erudite, or better yet, just stayed at his job. She craned her neck to look down, shook her head and said, "Look at that. Blood before faction."

LAURA MALLALIEU recently graduated from Rutgers University with her BA in English and a minor in Philosophy. She will not be jumping out of a moving train any time soon, but may soon be going to graduate school for her PhD, which in her opinion, is much scarier. She admires the Abnegation faction but would probably be an Erudite since she loves learning, chocolate cake, and the way she looks in fake glasses. She is taking her Erudite ways into the classroom, to teach fourth and fifth-grade English in Washington, DC.

TRIP MCCROSSIN teaches in the Philosophy Department at Rutgers University, where he works on, among other things, the nature, history, and legacy of the Enlightenment. There's some disagreement, it seems, about the collaborative nature of his classes. "How do they get anything done?" some object. "They don't care about efficiency," others say. "They care about agreement. Watch."

NICOLAS MICHAUD hasn't been able to find a home in any one field of knowledge. He likes to think this makes him Divergent. But he might just be easily distracted.

JORDAN PASCOE teaches philosophy at Manhattan College. She lives with her husband, dog, and three kids deep in the factionless section of Brooklyn, although everyone secretly suspects that the dog might be Amity.

DEBORAH PLESS got her degree in Philosophy from Hamilton College, and a degree in Creative Writing from New York Film Academy. She's since abandoned both of these pursuits in favor of seeking fame and glory on the Internet. Unfortunately, she's a blogger. She writes regularly for www.KissMyWonderWoman.com, and has contributed to *Doctor Who and Philosophy*, *Futurama and Philosophy*, *Representing 9/11*, and other books. She likes to think she'd pick Abnegation if given the choice, but she'd probably be seduced by the acoustic guitars and maxi skirts of Amity. She's not proud of this.

MARJORIE RHINE teaches English at the University of Wisconsin-Whitewater (not too far from Chicago!). She has published numerous articles on twentieth-century fiction. She lives in Madison, Wisconsin, with her husband and teenage daughter. Marjorie sometimes fantasizes that she most belongs in the Amity faction—wearing long hippie skirts, growing vegetables, and enjoying bread that puts everyone in a good mood. However, her daughter insists that Marjorie would absolutely be in the Erudite faction. After all, Marjorie was the kid who always read the most books in reading programs at the summer library, and she stills co-exists with far too many books!

KYLE A. SCHENKEWITZ holds an MA in Philosophy from the University of Southern Mississippi and a PhD in Historical Theology from Saint Louis University. His research examines how early Christian monastics cultivated virtue in their ascetic performances. He lives with his family as Factionless, though he exhibits the habituated traits of Candor and enjoys the simple pleasures of gardening and beer in Amity.

JESSICA SEYMOUR is a PhD candidate from Southern Cross University in Australia. Her research interests include children's and young adult literature, popular culture, and fan studies. She shows an aptitude for Amity and Erudite because, while she would adore the chance to investigate the Erudite compound's library, she disapproves of experimenting on humans.

JESSICA WATKINS has always been distraught by one-sided thinking. Maybe it's because, like Tris, she never quite fit in, and was frustrated and bored when she tried. Either way, her greatest adventure is working with young people whose divergent thinking inspires and gives her hope for a future far brighter than the one Beatrice was born into. She'd like to give special thanks to four of them—Nelay, Sean, Sarah, and Neil—for sharing those brilliant thoughts while brainstorming for her chapter in this volume.

Index

POPULAR CULTURE AND PHILOSOPHY®

DOCTOR WHO

AND PHILOSOPHY
BIGGER ON THE INSIDE

POLICE BOX

EDITED BY COURTLAND LEWIS AND PAULA SMITHKA